SRA Art Connections

Level 4

Authors

Rosalind Ragans, Ph.D., Senior Author

Willis Bing Davis

Tina Farrell

Jane Rhoades Hudak, Ph.D.

Gloria McCoy

Bunyan Morris

Nan Yoshida

Contributing Writer

Jackie Ellett

ART
SOURCE
ARTSOURCE

The Music Center of Los Angeles County

SRA McGraw-Hill

Columbus, Ohio

A Division of The McGraw·Hill Companies

SRA/McGraw-Hill

A Division of The **McGraw·Hill** Companies

Send all inquiries to:
SRA/McGraw-Hill
250 Old Wilson Bridge Road
Suite 310
Worthington, OH 43085

ISBN 0-02-688318-X

1 2 3 4 5 6 7 8 9 VHP 02 01 00 99 98 97

Authors

Senior Author
Rosalind Ragans, Ph.D.
Associate Professor Emerita,
Georgia Southern University

Willis Bing Davis,
Head of Art Department,
Central State University, Ohio

Tina Farrell,
Associate Director
of Visual and Performing Arts,
Clear Creek Independent School
District, Texas

Jane Rhoades Hudak,
Ph.D. Professor
of Art Teacher Education,
Georgia Southern University

Gloria McCoy,
K–12 Art Supervisor,
Spring Branch Independent School
District, Texas

Bunyan Morris,
Art Teacher,
Laboratory School,
Georgia Southern University

Nan Yoshida,
Former Art Supervisor,
Los Angeles Unified School
District, California

Contributors

ARTSOURCE Music, Dance, Theater Lessons
The Music Center of Los Angeles
County Education Division, Los
Angeles, California

More About Aesthetics
Richard W. Burrows, Executive
Director, Institute for Arts Education,
San Diego, California

Safe Use of Art Materials
Mary Ann Boykin, Visiting Lecturer,
Art Education; Director, The Art
School for Children and Young Adults,
University of Houston-Clear Lake,
Houston, Texas

Museum Education
Marilyn JS Goodman, Director of
Education, Solomon R. Guggenheim
Museum, New York, New York
National Museum of Women in the Arts Collection
National Museum of Women in the
Arts, Washington, DC

Reviewers

Mary Ann Boykin
Visiting Lecturer, Art Education;
Director, The Art School for Children
and Young Adults
University of Houston-Clear Lake
Houston, TX

Wendy M. Fries
Teacher
Kings River School
Kings River Union School District
Kingsburg, CA

Judy Gong
Multi-age Classroom Teacher
Pacific Elementary School
Lincoln Unified School District
Stockton, CA

Lori Groendyke Knutti
Art Educator
Harrison Street Elementary School
Big Walnut Elementary School
Sunbury, OH

Patsy Greenway
Art Specialist
Foerster Elementary School
Houston Independent School District
Houston, TX

Student Activity Testers

Richard McCloskey

Erica Akin

Eric Akin

Anthony Ciccone

TABLE OF CONTENTS

Unit 1  Line

Unit 2  Shape, Rhythm, and Movement

Table of Contents
(continued)

Unit 3 Color and Value

Unit 4 Form

Table of Contents
(continued)

Unit 5 Space and Texture

Unit 6 Balance, Harmony, Variety, Emphasis, and Unity

Table of Contents
(continued)

More About . . .

What Is Art?

Art is made by people

to communicate ideas.
to express our deepest feelings.
to satisfy our need for well-designed objects.

Art is . . .

Painting is color applied to a surface.

Miriam Shapiro. (American). *Pas de Deux.* 1986. Acrylic and fabric on canvas. 90 x 96 inches. Collection: Dr. and Mrs. A. Acinapusa/Courtesy Steinbaum Krauss Gallery, New York, New York.

Sculpture is art that fills up space.

Henry Moore. (British). *Family Group.* 1948–49. Bronze. $59\frac{1}{4}$ x $46\frac{1}{2}$ inches. The Museum of Modern Art, New York, New York. A. Longer Goodyear Fund. Photograph © 1998 The Museum of Modern Art.

Drawing is the process of making art with lines.

Katsushika Hokusai. (Japanese). *Boy with a Flute.* Ink on paper. $4\frac{1}{2}$ x $6\frac{1}{2}$ inches. Courtesy of the Freer Gallery of Art, Smithsonian Institution, Washington, DC.

Architecture is the art of designing and constructing buildings.

Artist unknown. (French). *Chartres Cathedral.* c. 1160. Chartres, Ile de France, France.

Printmaking is a process in which an original image is transferred from one prepared surface to another.

Katsushika Hokusai. (Japanese). *Print from 36 Views of Mount Fuji.* 1823–29. Colored woodcut. $10\frac{1}{8}$ x 15 inches. Metropolitan Museum of Art, New York, New York.

Photography is the act of capturing an image of light on film.

Jessica Hines. (American). *Spirit of Place Series #26.* Hand-colored, selectively toned silver print. 20 x 24 inches. Courtesy of Jessica Hines.

Ceramic objects are made from clay.

Artist unknown. (Chinese). *Architectural Model.* Western Han Dynesty. 206 B.C.–A.D. 8. Pottery with traces of paint, grey clay. 48 inches high. Philadelphia Museum of Art, Philadelphia, Pennsylvania.

Clothing design is the art of designing and making clothes.

Artist unknown. Osage, (American). *Osage Woman's Wedding Dress.* Cloth, ribbon, German silver, feather plumes, and beads. 120.1 cm long. Courtesy of the Smithsonian National Museum of the American Indian, NY. Photo by David Heald.

. . . and much more.

Art is a language.

The words of the language are the elements of art.

Line

Shape

Color

VALUE

SPACE

FORM

TEXTURE

Artists organize these words, or elements, using the principles of art.

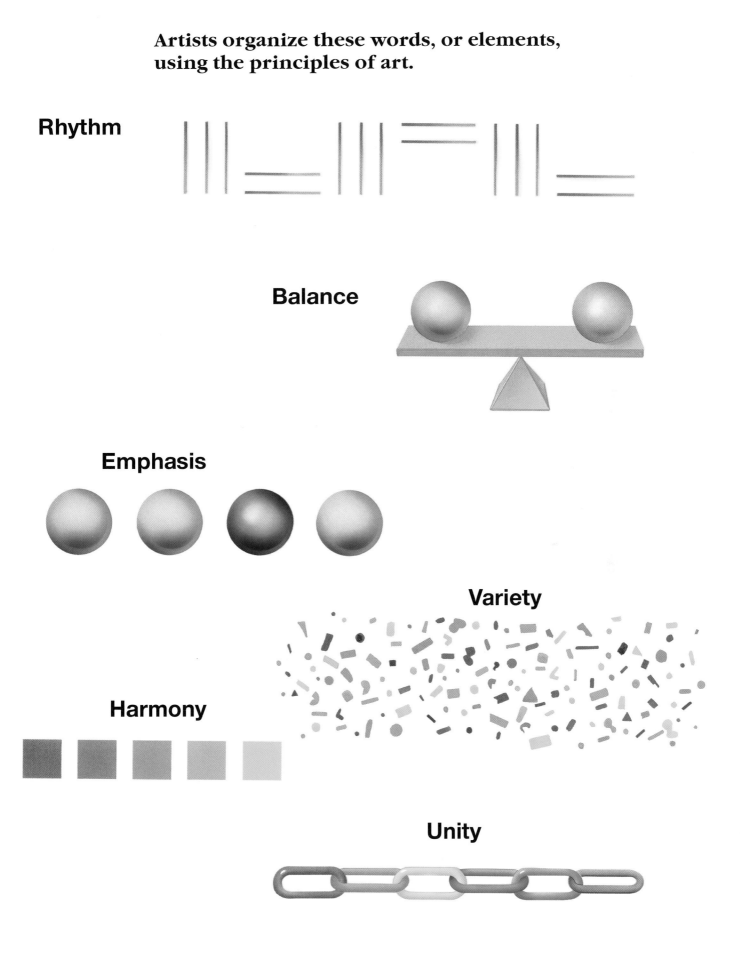

Rhythm

Balance

Emphasis

Variety

Harmony

Unity

Every work of art has three parts.

They are

SUBJECT

The subject is the objects you can recognize. If a work has no objects, the elements of art become the subject.

COMPOSITION

The composition is how the elements and principles are organized in the art work.

CONTENT

The content is the message or meaning of the artwork. If the work is functional, such as a chair or clothing, then the content is the function of the object.

Enrique Grau. (Colombian). *Nino con Paraguas*. 1964. Oil on canvas. 102 x 122 cm. Collection of the Art Museum of the Americas, Organization of American States.

Allan Houser. (American). *Coming of Age.* 1977. Bronze edition. $7\frac{1}{2}$ x $15\frac{1}{2}$ x 7 inches. Denver Art Museum, Denver, Colorado.

Artist unknown. (Chinese). *Carved Lacquer Circular Tray.* (Song Dynasty). Black, red, and yellow lacquer on wood. $2\frac{1}{16}$ x $13\frac{3}{4}$ inches. Courtesy of the Arthur M. Sackler Gallery, Smithsonian Institution, Washington, DC.

George Catlin. (American). *Buffalo Bull's Back Fat, Head Chief, Blood Tribe.* 1932. Oil on fabric mounted on aluminum. 29 x 24 inches. National Museum of American Art, Washington, DC, Art Resource, NY.

In which work of art do you think the subject matter is very important?

In which artwork do you think composition is most important?

Which work seems to have the strongest message? Explain?

Which artwork's meaning relates to its function?

An Introduction to
Line

Artists use a variety of lines to create artwork.

Utagawa Hiroshige. (Japanese). *Grounds of Kameido Tenjin Shrine.* 1856. Woodcut. 34 × 22.3 cm. Cincinnati Art Museum, OH. Gift of Charles Elam.

Artists use **lines** in drawings, paintings, and sculpture to create shapes and movement.

- What types of lines do you see in the print by Utagawa Hiroshige? What type of line do you see more than once?

- What shapes or lines look like they are moving in this print?

- Which side does it seem like you are standing on to view the art?

- Where do you see outlines in Utagawa's print?

Artist Profile

Cat in the Window.

Utagawa Hiroshige was born in Japan in 1797. He was named Andō. When he was 14, he began studying printmaking under Utagawa Toyohiro. A year later he graduated and adopted the name Utagawa. He is known for his landscapes and prints of people and nature.

Utagawa Hiroshigi and other artists use lines to help them create shapes and movement in a work of art. In this unit you will learn and practice the techniques that artists use to create lines in their artwork. Here are the topics you will study:

- Types of Lines
- Gestures
- Observation Drawing
- Contour Lines

Lines in Art

Artists use many different kinds of lines to create artwork.

Joseph Stella. (American). *The Great White Way I.* 1920. Oil and tempera on canvas. $88\frac{1}{2} \times 54$ inches. Newark Museum of Art, Newark, New Jersey.

The artists on these two pages used lines in different ways. Joseph Stella used strong lines to represent New York City. Jaune Quick-to-See Smith's painting uses loose brush strokes to reflect her feelings about the environment. The symbols in her painting are similar to symbols in the ancient Native American petroglyphs (rock drawings).

Jaune Quick-to-See Smith. (American). *Rainbow.* 1989. Oil and mixed-media on canvas.
66 × 84 inches. Private Collection/Courtesy Steinbaum Krauss Gallery, New York, New York.

Look closely at both works of art to find the different kinds of lines.

- ✓ Find five different line directions.
- ✓ Look for thick and thin lines.
- ✓ Where do you see rough and smooth lines?
- ✓ Can you find broken and solid lines?
- ✓ What's hiding in the brown line in *Rainbow*?

SEEING LIKE AN ARTIST

Look at line designs on your classmates' clothes. Can you find lines similar to those in both paintings?

Using Lines

A **line** is a mark drawn by a tool such as a pencil, pen, or paintbrush as it moves across a surface. Artists use lines to describe how an object looks. You looked at two paintings that are made of five different kinds of lines with four different line variations on the previous page.

Here are some different types of lines:

 A **vertical** line moves up and down.

 A **horizontal** line moves from side to side or left to right.

 A **diagonal** line moves from corner to corner.

 **Zigzags** are diagonal lines that connect.

 **Curved** lines bend and change direction slowly.

Practice

Working in small groups, role-play each of the line types and variations. Let your classmates guess which line your group is illustrating.

Decide Was one line harder to role-play than others?

1. Divide into small groups and choose a line to role-play.

2. Role-play your line to your classmates. Can they guess what you are illustrating?

Christopher Cornelison. Age 8. *Save Our Rain Forest*. Colored markers.

What kind of lines did this student artist use to show how he feels about the rain forest?

Create

What emotions do you feel when you think about a cause that concerns you? Create a poster using different kinds of lines and a symbol to represent your cause.

1. Think about a cause that concerns you, such as pollution. Write a short slogan or message that expresses your concerns.

2. Design a poster about your cause. Use the different kinds of lines and line variations you saw in the artworks. Plan a way to work your slogan into a design like Jaune Quick-to-See Smith did.

Describe Name the objects and the slogan in your poster.

Analyze List the different lines you used. How did you make your slogan fit the design?

Interpret Does your poster express your concern? Do your friends understand what you are trying to say?

Decide Did you use the five different kinds of lines in your poster?

Gesture Drawing

Artists use the gesture drawings to capture
the feeling of motion.

Audrey Flack. (American).
Self-Portrait (*the Memory*). 1958
Oil on canvas. 50 × 34 inche
Art Museum Miami Univ
Oxford, Ohio.

Look at the artwork on these two pages. *Self-P*
(the Memory) was painted in 1958 by Audrey Fla
when she was an art student. About 150 years earlier,
Fragonard created his drawing as one of a series of drawings
to illustrate a story. Although both artists used different
materials in their artwork, they both used quickly drawn lines
to express movement.

Jean-Honoré Fragonard. (French). *Rodomonte and Mandricardo State their Case before Agramante.* 1780s. Pen and brown and gray wash over black chalk on cream-laid paper. $15\frac{1}{2} \times 10\frac{1}{4}$ inches. Museum of Fine Arts, Houston, Texas.

Look closely at both works of art and find the lines that show movement.

✓ Find a repeated line that represents movement.

✓ Which figure seems to be the most lively? Which figure seems to be the calmest?

✓ Describe how detail is used or not used in each of the artworks.

✓ Compare the works of art. What similarities do you see? What differences?

SEEING LIKE AN ARTIST

Look around classroom how every moving. Not variety of gestu around you. How these movements show feelings?

Using Gesture

A **gesture** is an expressive movement. **Gesture lines** are quickly drawn to capture the movement of a person, animal, or object in a painting or drawing. You saw two works of art using the techniques needed to show gesture on the previous pages.

A **gesture sketch** is a quick sketch. When trying to capture the gesture of an object, quick sketches or action drawings are used. The idea is to capture the movement or action of the object as quickly as possible.

Repeated lines are used to give the feeling of movement or motion.

Repeated shapes, like hands or legs, also give the feeling of motion. The more times the shapes are repeated, the faster the motion looks.

Because gestures are used to capture movement, **minimal detail** is used in the rest of the drawing. Often detail is just suggested, like a line for a mouth or an eye.

Practice

Illustrate the three gesture techniques. Use crayon.

1. Choose one area of your classroom to draw. Make a quick sketch capturing the gestures of several of your classmates, like the gestures you saw in the Fragonard drawing.

2. Make sure your sketch has repeated lines, shapes, and very little detail.

Decide Did you use repeated lines and shapes and little detail? What did you find most difficult?

Anna Focks. Age 9. *Wild Gestures*. Crayon and tempera.

How did this student artist create the feeling of motion?

Create

How can you show action or motion in a drawing? Create the feeling of motion in a gesture drawing.

1. Think about how action is drawn. Many curved lines are used.

2. Take turns with classmates freezing in a movement for 30 seconds. Each time you draw a figure, change crayon color.

3. Repeat lines and shapes and let your figures overlap, filling the entire page.

Describe Describe the figures in your drawing.

Analyze Talk about the various gesture techniques that you used.

Interpret What type of feeling have you created in your drawing? What did you do that created this feeling? What kind of lines seem to represent action?

Decide Do you feel you successfully caught the gestures of your classmates?

Lesson 2

Observation Drawing

Artists often sketch scenes showing how people interact with each other and the environment.

Peter Bruegel the Elder. (Austrian). *Children's Games.* 1560. Oil on oakwood panel. $46\frac{1}{2} \times 63\frac{3}{8}$ inches. Kuntshistoriches Museus, Gemaeldegalerie, Vienna, Austria, photographed by Erich Lessing/Art Resource, NY.

Look at the paintings on these pages. *Children's Games* was painted by the artist Peter Bruegel and shows many children playing games in the sixteenth century. The *Endangered Species Mural* by Paul Goodnight also focuses on children. However, they are in a completely different environment.

Paul Goodnight. (American). *Endangered Species.* Acrylic. $2\frac{1}{2}$ x 5 feet.

Look closely at both artworks and notice how they show different ways of seeing action.

✓ How did the artists capture the poses of the children?

✓ Both artists portrayed children very differently moving in their environments. What different messages do you think the artists were sending us? What feelings do you get when you look at both pictures?

✓ How many different games can you find in the Breugel artwork?

SEEING LIKE AN ARTIST
Look around your classroom at your classmates. Notice how the people close to you look larger than the people far away.

Using Observation Drawing

An **observation drawing** is a drawing made while looking at a person or object. Artists draw figures or objects in relation to their surroundings, but the murals often show different points of view.

 **Bird's-Eye View**—Viewers feel they are looking down on a scene.

 **Ant's View**—Viewers feel they are looking up toward an object or figure.

 **Faraway**—Viewers feel they are standing far away from the scene.

 **Close-Up**—Viewers feel they are right next to the object or a part of the action in a picture.

Practice

Create sketches showing gesture. Use pencil.

1. Work in small groups. Take turns posing while the others make 30-second gesture drawings. Use different points of view.

2. Look at the gestures of the children in *Children's Games* for ideas.

Decide Were you able to capture the model's gesture in 30 seconds? Which point of view was easiest for you? What did you find the most difficult?

Zachary Harris. Age 9. *Having Fun.* Black marker.

How did this student artist capture action
in his drawing?

Create

**How can you best capture the action of a
group of children running and playing? Draw
a sketch by observing children at play.**

1. Think about repeating lines and shapes to
   draw the gestures.

2. Go to the school playground and watch all
   the action that is taking place.

3. Sketch a variety of gestures from a specific
   point of view. Show the gestures of the
   children and some of their environment. Fill
   the entire page, making sure to overlap your
   objects and use a variety of lines.

Describe Describe the people
and their environment.

Analyze Explain how you
captured the gestures in relation
to their environment.

Interpret Describe how your
selected viewpoint created a
certain feeling in your picture.

Decide Did you successfully draw
the gestures of the people in
relation to their environment?

Contour Lines

Artists use contour drawing to help them develop their ability to see and record objects.

Henri Matisse. (French). *Les glaieuls.* Study for *Poesies de Stephane Mallarme.* 1931-32. Pen and black ink. The Baltimore Museum of Art: The Cone Collection, formed by Dr. Claribel Cone and Miss Etta Cone of Baltimore, Maryland.

Henri Matisse made this pen-and-ink drawing of *Les glaieuls* in 1941. He focused on the outlines and ridges of the flower form, using only lines to define these edges. The print by Mark Uqayuittuq also uses lines to show or define the edges of the figure. Notice how line is used in both pieces of art. Do you see how these artists used contour lines to define the edges and ridges of the forms in their pictures?

Mark Uqayuittuq. Inuit (American). *Friendly Spirits*. 1972.
Stonecut and colored stencils. 1981. 49.9 × 59.1 cm.
Cincinnati Museum of Art, Cincinnati, Ohio.

Notice how the lines flow throughout both pictures, creating edges or contours.

 Where do you think the lines in each picture begin and end?

 Describe some of the lines you see.

 Often, lines can create a feeling. What mood was created using lines in each of these pictures?

 What areas are emphasized more than others? What techniques did the artists use to emphasize these areas?

S EEING LIKE
AN ARTIST

Closely observe objects in your environment. Notice changes in surface areas that would be defined as a contour in a drawing, such as fold lines in clothing, or open spaces in objects like scissors or a crate.

Using Contour Lines

The **contour** of an object or figure is its edge and surface ridges. Artists often make contour drawings of objects and use them as studies before making a painting or drawing. They also make blind contour drawings, which help them become more perceptive. Even if these drawings are not too accurate, making them develops an artist's ability to observe.

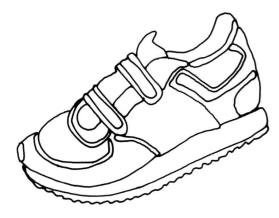

Contour Lines are lines that show the edges and surface ridges of an object.

A **blind contour drawing** is the type of drawing that is done by looking at the object being drawn and not at the paper. This can be done by following the edges and ridges of an object with your eyes as you slowly draw it with your pen. Try not to look at your paper, but concentrate on the object you are drawing. Do not lift your pen from the paper. Try to draw one continuous line.

Practice

Create a blind contour of your hand. Use felt-tip pen.

1. Look closely at your hand. Notice all the contours, the outer edges, the folds when you close your hand, and the lines around your knuckles.

2. Draw a blind contour of your hand, looking at it from one angle. Try to make your drawing one continuous line.

Decide Look closely at your blind contours. Were you able to draw all the folds and wrinkles? Did you use one continuous line? Do your drawings look like hands?

Nicole K. Chipi. Age 9. *REJ 13.* Fine-point marker.

What type of lines do you see in this student artist's blind contour drawing?

Create

How can you draw a picture without looking at your paper? Create a blind contour drawing of a model using a continuous line.

1. Do the objects and people around you have curved edges, straight edges, or both? Discuss contour lines and point out examples.

2. Now take turns modeling in five-minute poses. Draw one blind contour of a classmate. Allow your eye to move slowly along the edges, or contours, of the model as you slowly draw. Try to not lift your marker. Let it touch the paper at all times. Concentrate on the model without looking at your paper.

3. Add one or two objects that are next to the model in your drawing.

Describe Describe the types of lines you used to create your contour drawing.

Analyze Discuss how some lines gave energy or movement, while other lines were calm.

Interpret What kind of mood was created by your drawing?

Decide What strategies did you use to make your drawings successful? Did you improve as you did more contour drawings?

Thick and Thin Contour Lines

Artists use contour lines to show the edges of an object and surface ridges to separate areas within that object.

Benny Andrews. (American). *The Scholar.* 1974. Pen and ink on paper. 12 × 9 inches. Private Collection.

Notice how Benny Andrews used contour lines to define the edges and areas of the objects in his drawings. The artist used contour lines in both pictures to create edges, or contours, of various objects.

Benny Andrews. (American). *Patriots*. 1991. Pen and ink. $22\frac{1}{2}$ x 15 inches. Courtesy of the Cumberland Gallery.

Look closely at the contour lines.

- ✓ Describe some of the lines used in the pictures.

- ✓ Where do you see lines that look unbroken?

- ✓ How did the artist solve the problem of showing some objects close up and others far away?

- ✓ Are the lines all the same thickness or do they change? What effect does this have on the artworks?

Lesson 5

Using Thick and Thin Contour Lines

The purpose behind a contour drawing is to improve your **perception**, or the way you look or think about what you see. In **contour drawing**, your hand slowly draws across the paper at the same time your eye is slowly moving along the edges or contours of the object. Your pen is seldom lifted from the paper. Make sure you look at the object when you are drawing and only glance at your paper once in a while.

Some artists use contour lines to draw people, and others use them to draw **still lifes**. A still-life drawing is a picture of things that do not move. Artists like Benny Andrews consider the drawing the final project. Others create contour drawings to further explore an object before making a painting or final drawing. Often the artist will vary the line quality, making some lines thicker and darker than others. **Line variation** refers to the changes in the look of a line. Often artists will vary the thickness of their lines for emphasis.

Thick/Thin

Long Short

Rough/Smooth

Solid/Broken

Practice

Create a contour drawing of an object. Use felt-tip pen.

1. Look closely at an object. Notice all the contours. Look at how some lines are unbroken and some are of varying thicknesses.

2. Using pen, draw two views using the technique of contour drawing. Try to include thick and thin lines.

Decide Were you able to accurately draw your object from two points of view?

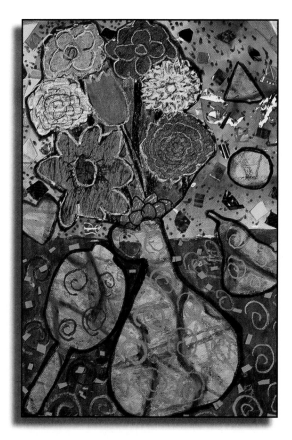

Jessica Philogene. Age 9. Felt-tip pen and oil pastel.

How did this student artist create a feeling of depth in her still life?

Create

How do contour lines help create an effective drawing? Create a still-life drawing using contour lines.

1. Look closely at the still life. Observe the areas or shapes formed by the contours. Notice that some objects are closer to you, while others are farther away. Some are partially hidden.

2. Make several quick sketches of the different parts.

3. Begin drawing. Allow your eye to move slowly along the edge of each object. Draw all important lines, varying the thickness of some lines.

Describe Describe how your lines and objects look.

Analyze Explain how you created the illusion of depth.

Interpret What similarities and differences do you see between this contour drawing and other drawings you have made?

Decide Evaluate your final contour drawing in comparison with other contour drawings you have done recently.

Flowing Lines

Some artists are able to create the final version of their artwork without making earlier sketches.

Katsushika Hokusai. (Japanese). *Boy with a Flute.* 1984. Ink on paper. $4\frac{1}{2} \times 6\frac{1}{4}$ inches.
Freer Gallery of Art, Smithsonian Institution, Washington, DC.

Look closely at the paintings on these two pages. Notice how Hokusai used repeated lines and concentrated on the contours of the objects. The lines are of various thicknesses. In the second work, the Chinese statesman Wang Ao wrote his poem in characters drawn with flowing lines. The artist Shen Zhou painted the branch of the pomegranate tree to illustrate the poem. Both artists worked directly on paper with ink.

Shen Zhou and **Wang Ao.** (Chinese). *Ode to the Pomegranate and Melon Vine.* ca. 1508–09. Hanging scroll, ink and color on paper. $58\frac{5}{8} \times 29\frac{3}{4}$ inches. The Detroit Institute of the Arts, Detroit, Michigan.

Study both artworks to see how the artists used painted lines to create flowing contours.

✓ Describe how the lines are used in the paintings.

✓ Are the lines all the same? Are some thicker than others?

✓ What do you think the child in the Hokusai drawing is feeling?

SEEING LIKE AN ARTIST

Look at the different brushes in your classroom. Which one would make the thinnest lines?

Using Flowing Lines

Artists create **observation brush drawings** as first sketches done with a brush and watercolors. This way, they begin with the same tools they use to finish their work. Often the first effort becomes the final version of the painting.

You can create **light lines** by adding more water to your watercolor paints, or **dark lines** by using less water.

To create a **thin line,** hold the brush vertically to the paper and touch the paper lightly with the tip of the brush.

To make a line **thick,** begin with a **thin line** and gradually press the brush down. Pull up again to make it thinner.

Practice

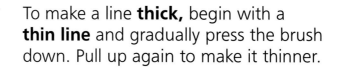

Create a thick to thin line. Use watercolors and a pointed brush.

1. Fill your brush with paint. Use the point of your brush for thin lines and press gently on your brush for thick lines.

2. Practice using different pressure on your brush to make lines change.

Decide Do you better understand how to create thick and thin lines?

What mood has this student artist created?

Create

How can your first sketch develop into your final version? Draw a person in a complex setting using a variety of lines.

1. Think about the variety of lines used to create contours in objects and people around you.

2. Make several quick sketches from various points of view to help you select one area of the subject to paint. Be sure to include a variety of lines in your sketches.

3. Begin by painting the contour lines of the person. Then, add the objects around the person. Fill some areas of your drawing with paint.

Describe Describe the person and the objects in your painting, and then describe the types of lines you drew.

Analyze Compare this painting to your contour drawing. Were some of the line qualities the same?

Interpret Discuss the mood that was created by using watercolors.

Decide Do you feel the painting was successful? Why or why not? What would you do differently next time?

Lines in Pantomime

The Chameleons: Sharon Diskin and Keith Berger.

mimes never speak. They communicate with the movements of their bodies and the expressions on their faces. Think about how you look when you are sad. Your mouth turns down. Your shoulders slump. You stare at the floor. Mimes communicate feelings by exaggerating movements like these. Their movements create curved, straight, and diagonal lines.

What To Do

Use the focus and expression of your eyes to communicate.

Materials

None

1. List several situations in which your eyes could tell a story. Examples: watching a tennis match, a plane take-off, a scary movie, or a spider crawling near your toes.

2. Choose a situation. Practice using your eyes to respond to it.

3. Work with a partner. Each do your own interpretation of a situation at the same time. Use only your eyes and head to show what is happening.

4. Now respond to the situation using your body. You can stand, walk, lean, turn away, or sit, but keep communicating with your eyes. Your movements will create straight, continuous, broken, curved, and diagonal lines.

Describe Tell what you did to communicate the situation with your eyes.

Analyze Identify the different types of lines that you formed.

Interpret Explain how your movements expressed different moods.

Decide How well did you succeed in showing a feeling or situation by using your eyes?

Extra Credit

Try miming other situations with a partner.
Perform them for others.

Line

Reviewing Main Ideas

The lessons in this unit cover the techniques that artists use when creating lines.

1. **Line** is the path created by a moving point or dot. There are many types of lines, such as curved or zigzag, but only three directions in which all lines can move.

   - **Horizontal** lines move from side to side or left to right.

   - **Diagonal** lines slant from corner to corner.

   - **Vertical** lines move up and down.

   - **Zigzags** are diagonal lines that connect and change direction sharply.

   - **Curved** lines bend and change directions slowly.

2. An **observation drawing** is made while looking at a person or object.

3. A **gesture sketch** is a quick sketch or action drawing of an object or person done as quickly as possible.

4. A **contour** is the outline or edges of an object or figure.

5. **Line variation** refer to changes in the looks of a line.

Andrew Wyeth. (American). *The Chambered Nautilus.* 1956.

Summing Up

The Chambered Nautilus was painted by American artist Andrew Wyeth in 1956. In this painting, Wyeth used a variety of lines.

- Has Wyeth used all five different types of lines? Try to locate an example of each one in his painting.
- Where are lines that change from thin to thick?
- Where do you see an example of a gesture drawing?
- Do you see any contour lines? Describe them.

Lines are important to artists because they communicate how an object looks, feels, and moves.

Let's Visit a Museum

The Wadsworth Atheneum in Hartford, Connecticut, is the oldest public art museum in America. It has about 50,000 artworks from the United States and other countries. Bronze pieces from ancient Egypt, Greece, and Rome and paintings from the past 400 years can be found there. The museum also has the Amistad Collection, which is a history of African American culture. The museum has many programs and activities for people of all ages and interests who love art.

The Wadsworth Atheneum

An Introduction to
Shape, Rhythm, and Movement

Shape, rhythm, and movement are used by artists to add variety and interest to an artwork.

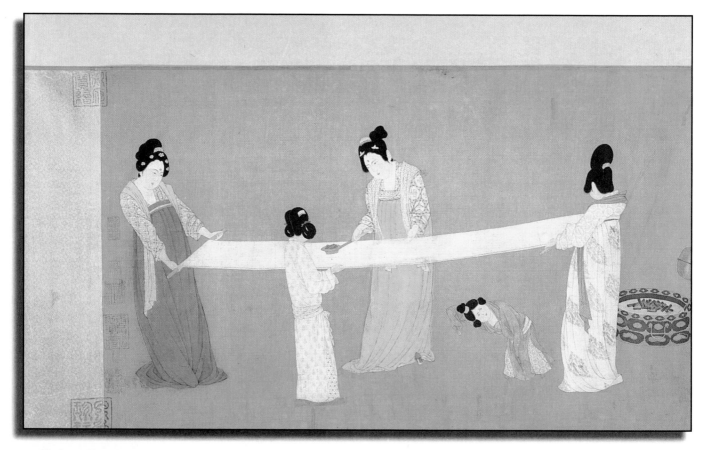

Artist unknown. (Chinese). Court *Ladies Preparing Newly Woven Silk.* (Detail). 1082–1135. Handscroll: ink, colors, and gold on silk. 37 × 145.3 cm. Chinese and Japanese Special Fund Courtesy of Museum of Fine Arts, Boston, Massachusetts.

Artists use **shapes** to represent forms found in nature and forms created by people.

- What types of shapes do you see in the women's hair, and their bodies in their clothing, and in the box on the pictures right.

Often artists will repeat shapes, lines, or colors to create a pattern or **rhythm** in their artwork.

- What shapes and colors create a rhythm?

Some artists will repeat a shape or stop a form in motion to create the illusion of **visual movement.**

- How does the artist capture the movement or action of the women and girls working with the silk?

Silk Embroidery

The tapestry you see on this page was part of a robe created for a Chinese emperor or a member of his royal court. It is made of silk and gold threads sewn onto the silk. Silk tapestry fabric was extremely precious. It was probably created by a female artist who worked for the emperor. Silk was first produced in China more than 4,000 years ago. It comes from the silkworm moth. For centuries, the collecting and weaving of silk was a secret process.

Artists like the Chinese silk makers use shape, rhythm, and movement to help them create a work of art. In this unit you will learn and practice techniques to create the feeling of rhythm and movement in an artwork. You will also review types of shapes. Here are the topics you will study:

- Geometric Shapes
- Free-Form Shapes
- Rhythm
- Visual Movement

Geometric Shapes in Art

Artists use geometric and free-form shapes to organize two-dimensional works of art.

George Catlin. (American). *Buffalo Bull's Back Fat, head chief, Blood Tribe* (Blackfoot). 1832. Oil on fabric mounted on aluminum. 29 × 24 inches. Gift of Mrs. Joseph Harrison, Jr. National Museum of American Art, Washington, DC, Art Resource, NY.

Both paintings on these pages show how artists use geometric and free-form shapes to organize their work. Notice how Catlin's *Buffalo Bull's Back Fat* uses an almost rectangular shape for the lock of hair falling on the forehead. Catlin was very concerned with the disappearing Native American cultures, and so he documented their life in many paintings. John Biggers's *Shotgun Third Ward* is made of free-form and geometric shapes. Notice how Catlin's geometric shapes are not as obvious as Biggers's.

John Biggers. (American). *Shotgun Third Ward.* 1966. Oil on canvas. 76.2 × 121.9 cm.
National Museum of American Art, Washington, DC, Art Source, NY

Both artists use geometric shapes in their artwork.

 Where are the circles, squares, and triangles in these works?

☑ What other geometric shapes do you see?

☑ What things do these shapes represent?

☑ Where do you use free-form shapes?

☑ Looking at both artworks, what moods do you feel?

☑ Both artists used their art to tell a story. What stories do you think these two works of art tell?

SEEING LIKE AN ARTIST

Look out a window, around your classroom, or through this book. Notice how the objects you see are made of a variety of shapes. Make a list of three items and describe the geometric shapes needed to draw them.

Using Geometric Shapes

Geometric shapes are shapes that can be described and measured in mathematical terms. They can be drawn with a ruler or compass. The geometric shapes in this lesson are **two-dimensional**, which means they are flat. You can measure the length and width of a rectangle or the circumference and diameter of a circle.

Here are five geometric shapes.

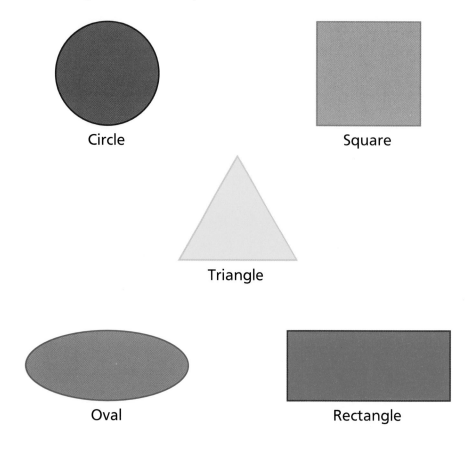

Circle

Square

Triangle

Oval

Rectangle

Practice

Create a drawing of your hand using only geometric shapes. Use a marker.

1. Notice how each area of your hand can be represented with a geometric shape. For instance, a part of your finger could be drawn as a rectangle.

2. Create two drawings of your hand. Using geometric shapes, draw your hand from different angles.

Decide Were you able to draw your hand using geometric shapes? Does your finished picture look like a human hand?

Unit **2**

Chris Gunter. Age 9. *The Cool One.* Mixed media.

What are three geometric shapes in this student artist's collage?

Create

What shapes are the people, places, and things around you? Create a collage based on a theme.

1. Think about a theme for your collage. Make some quick sketches, using geometric and free-form shapes.

2. Draw your best sketch. Add collected materials.

3. Before you glue, arrange your collage until you find a design you like best. Use as many geometric shapes as you can. Fill the background with color.

Describe Describe the subject matter and materials of your collage.

Analyze Where did you use geometric and free-form shapes? Why did you choose the colors and shapes you used in your collage?

Interpret Give your work a title.

Decide Do you feel you were successful in using shapes to create objects in your collage? If you were to do it over, what would you change?

Free-Form Shapes

Sometimes artists use free-form shapes to represent objects found in nature.

Stuart Davis. (American). *Composition*. 1935. Oil on canvas. $22\frac{1}{4} \times 30\frac{1}{8}$ inches. National Museum of American Art, Washington, DC/Art Resource/© Stuart Davis/Licensed by VAGA, New York, NY

There are many free-form shapes in the two paintings on these pages. Stuart Davis painted this still life, *Composition,* in 1935. He simplified what he saw and created geometric and free-form shapes. Minnie Evans used free-form shapes in her painting to communicate her dreams. Look for the free-form shapes in these paintings. Also look for geometric shapes.

Minnie Evans. (American). *Design Made at Airlie Gardens.* 1967. Oil and mixed media on canvas. 50.5 × 60.6 cm. National Museum of American Art, Washington, DC, Art Resource, NY.

Both paintings are made of a variety of shapes.

✓ What types of shapes do you see most often in both paintings?

✓ What are some ways that these artists created these shapes?

✓ Describe some of the free-form and geometric shapes that you see.

✓ Both paintings have a certain mood. Describe it.

✓ Do these paintings remind you of anything you have seen or experienced before? If so, what?

SEEING LIKE AN ARTIST
Think about the various objects in nature that are made of free-form shapes.

Using Free-Form Shapes

Free-form shapes are irregular and uneven. A free-form shape is any shape that isn't a geometric shape. Free-form shapes are sometimes called organic shapes because they occur in nature. They can also be created from the imagination.

These are examples of solid and outlined free-form shapes.

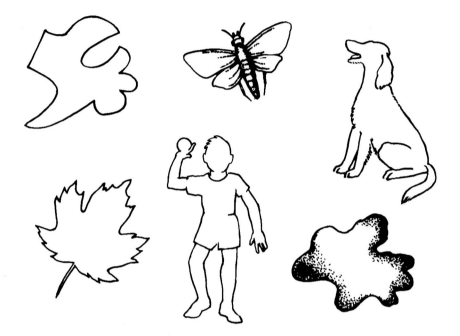

Practice

Draw a silhouette using free-form shapes. Use a felt-tip marker.

1. A **silhouette** is the shape of a shadow. Many silhouettes are free-form shapes.

2. Look at objects that are made with free-form shapes. Draw a silhouette of one of these objects. Color it solid.

Decide Show your silhouette to classmates. Can they recognize the object from its shape?

Nate Byers. Age 9. *Deep Sea.* Dustless chalk and watercolors.

How would this painting "feel" different if the student artist used geometric shapes?

Create

Have you ever pretended to be in a different world or a city under the sea? Use free-form shapes to create a fantasy painting.

1. Think about how common objects would look in your new environment. Sketch some of the objects, changing them into free-form shapes.

2. Choose several of your sketches to include in your fantasy painting. First, draw your picture. Then, fill your scene with color.

3. Use a small brush or a marker to add details.

Describe Describe the objects in your painting. Was it easy to use free-form shapes to create them?

Analyze Did you change geometric shapes to free-form shapes?

Interpret Give your work a title that expresses its mood.

Decide Were you successful in using free-form shapes to represent objects?

Visual Rhythm

**When artists repeat a line, shape, or color,
they create visual rhythm in their art.**

Artist unknown. (Africa). Untitled. 1983. Bombololu Handicraft
Center. Mombossa, Kenya. Woodblock print. Gold print on black.
Private Collection.

The two images on these pages are related to
printmaking. The woodblock is used to stamp cloth.
Notice the repeated lines and shapes that are used in the
cloth and the woodblock. The artists have created rhythm by
repeating motifs.

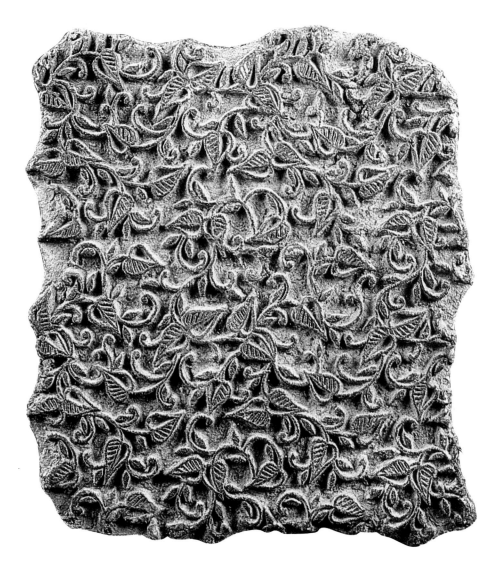

Artist unknown. (India). Woodblock. Late 1800s. Antique woodblock. Private Collection.

Study both artworks for examples of rhythm.

- What type of material was used to create the stamper for the motif?

- What types of repetition do you see?

- The African cloth has a complicated motif. What do you think these designs represent?

- What mood do you feel when you look at the cloth?

SEEING LIKE AN ARTIST
Look around you and see if you recognize any visual rhythms in your classroom.

Recognizing Rhythm

Rhythm occurs when artists repeat lines, shapes, or colors in their work to create a feeling of movement. In music, rhythm is heard as a beat. **Visual rhythm** is rhythm you receive through your eyes rather than through your ears.

A **motif** is something visual that is repeated in rhythm. The motif can be the same each time, or it may vary. In a grocery store, each can on a shelf full of canned goods is a motif, even if the labels vary.

Random rhythm has motifs that appear in no apparent order, with irregular spaces in between.

Regular rhythm has identical motifs and equal amounts of space between them.

Alternating rhythm is when the motif is changed in some way or a second motif is introduced.

One motif   Two motifs

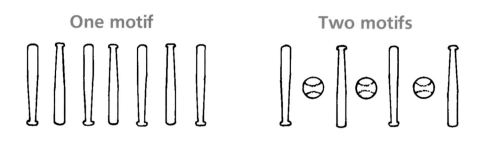

Practice

Arrange classroom objects into rhythms.

Decide Did other groups recognize which rhythms you illustrated?

Ashley Hough. Age 9. *Starry Night*. Stamp and tempera.

What would be the next stamp in each of this student artist's rhythms?

Create

How can you use one motif to print different rhythms? Create a printing stamp.

1. Think about a design for an interesting motif. Draw several ideas and choose your favorite.

2. Divide a piece of paper into three sections. Print a random rhythm in one section and a regular rhythm in another section. In the third, create an alternating rhythm.

Describe Describe the motif you created and the process you used to make your print.

Analyze How many different kinds of rhythms did you use? Explain the differences in the rhythms.

Interpret Pretend each section is visual music, and give each one a title.

Decide Did you illustrate each rhythm correctly?

Flowing Rhythm

Artists express flowing rhythm in a variety of ways.

Katsushika Hokusai. (Japanese). *Kajikaawa* from *The Thirty-six Views of Fuji.*
1828–29. Colored woodcut. 10$\frac{1}{2}$ × 15 inches. Metropolitan Museum of Art,
New York, New York.

Both works of art explore flowing rhythm. Look closely at the print of *Kajikaawa* by Katsushika Hokusai. This woodcut was made more than 160 years ago. Notice how Hokusai captured the flowing rhythm in the waves. The bronze sculpture *Coming of Age* by Allen Houser was made in 1977. Notice how Houser created the feeling of movement through the flowing rhythm of the lines in the girl's hair.

Allen Houser. (American). *Coming of Age.* 1977. Bronze. $12\frac{1}{2} \times 15\frac{1}{2} \times 7$ inches. Courtesy of Denver Art Museum, Denver, Colorado.

Study both artworks to answer these questions.

- ✓ What kinds of lines do you see most often in both artworks? Where are the lines located?

- ✓ Where do you see flowing rhythms in the works of art? What kinds of lines help create them?

- ✓ Describe the subject of each artwork.

- ✓ Why do you think these artists chose these particular subjects for their artworks?

SEEING LIKE AN ARTIST

Think of places where you can find flowing rhythms in nature.

Creating Rhythm

One way to create rhythm in a work of art is by repeating curved lines or shapes. This type of rhythm is known as **flowing rhythm**. There are no sudden changes in lines or breaks in the movement.

Curved lines, like the ocean waves you saw in Hokusai's print and the hair in Houser's sculpture, create flowing rhythms.

Free-form shapes that are repeated can sometimes create a flowing rhythm.

Practice

Create an original design using flowing rhythms. Use black marker.

1. Flowing rhythms can be the change of tides, the bark on a tree, or rolling hills. Think about flowing rhythms in nature.

2. Choose an item with a flowing rhythm and create a close-up of a part of that item using repeated lines. Think about how it might look under a microscope and try to reproduce that idea.

Decide What lines and shapes did you use in your design to portray flowing rhythm?

Schansa Blackburn. Age 9. *At the Water's Edge.* Construction paper.

If the student artist added drawn flowing lines between the cut lines, how would the rhythm change?

Create

How does the wind shape and change lines and forms in nature? Create a flowing rhythm design.

1. Think about how lines can show rhythm. Cut a variety of curving lines and long, flowing free-form shapes from paper.

2. Arrange the cut papers until you get a flowing rhythm design you like. Then, glue the papers down.

Describe Name the types of lines and shapes you used.

Analyze Why is the color blue a good choice for this flowing rhythm?

Interpret What would be a good title to explain your work?

Decide Did you successfully create a flowing rhythm?

Rhythm and Movement

Artists use rhythm in many ways to create visual movement.

Joan Mirò. (Spanish). *Symbols and Love Constellations of a Woman.* 1941. Watercolor and gouache 45.6 × 38 cm. Art Institute of Chicago, Chicago, Illinois. Gift of Gilbert W. Chapman/© 1998 Artists Rights Society (ARS), New York/ADAGP, Paris.

Both paintings are **nonobjective paintings**. They have no recognizable subject matter. Both paintings on these pages illustrate visual movement. Both artists used repeated lines, shapes, and colors to create a random rhythm. When your eyes follow rhythm in a work of art, you experience visual movement. Do both works seem to move visually at the same speed?

Richard Pousette-Dart. (American). *Within the Room*. 1942. Oil on canvas. 36 × 60 inches. © 1996 Collection of the Whitney Museum of American Art, New York, New York/Promised 50th Anniversary Gift of the Artist.

Study both paintings to see how rhythm was used to create the feeling of movement.

- What types of lines and shapes do you see? What colors do you see?

- Explain how the artists created rhythm in the paintings.

- What types of rhythm were used in each—random, regular, alternating, or flowing?

- When rhythm is used, it creates the feeling of movement, such as fast or slow. Explain the way the movement feels as you study these paintings.

- What other types of feelings do you get when you look at these paintings?

SEEING LIKE AN ARTIST

Look around you. Notice the number of things that move or can be moved with your help.

Communicating Visual Movement

Our world is in constant motion. When a flower blooms, the wind blows, or a ball is hit through the air, **movement** occurs. Artists have been using rhythm to show the feeling of **visual movement** in art for a very long time.

Artists use lines to control your eye movement. This kind of line can be the repetition of any movement that pulls your eyes through the work.

This is not a line in the usual sense. It is an **implied line**. That is, it is a series of points that are automatically connected by the viewer's eyes.

Practice

Plan and present short skits to illustrate the rhythm of visual movement.

Decide Did each group present a skit that showed movement? How many skits illustrated implied line?

Aubrey Silva. Age 9. *Color Reflections.* Oil pastel and watercolor.

How has this student artist created visual movement?

Create

How can lines, shapes, and colors show movement? Create a nonobjective painting to illustrate visual movement.

1. Think about how you can illustrate visual movement. Fold a sheet of paper into eight equal sections. In each section, illustrate a different action or movement using line and shape. Use rhythms to create visual movement.

2. On another sheet of paper, use oil pastels to combine several of your designs. Vary the thickness of your lines.

3. Using watercolors, add more color to your design and watch the oil pastels resist the paint. Fill the paper with color.

Describe What are some of the lines, shapes, and colors you see? Are some lines or shapes overlapping?

Analyze What did you repeat to create the feeling of visual movement?

Interpret Think of a popular song that expresses the mood of your design.

Decide Do you feel your painting successfully illustrated visual movement?

Lesson 5

Visual Movement

Artists may draw the main action of a story
or poem, or draw a series of actions.

Marc Chagall. (Russian). *Birthday.* Oil on cardboard. $31\frac{3}{4} \times 39\frac{1}{4}$ inches. The Museum
of Modern Art, New York, New York. Acquired through the Lillie P. Bliss Bequest
Photograph © 1998 The Museum of Modern Art, New York. © 1998 Artists Rights
Society (ARS), New York/ADAGP, Paris.

Each of these paintings tells a part of a story. Each
shows the main action or event in the story. Marc
Chagall's painting of himself and his wife Bella portrays the
most important part of a birthday story in a dreamlike way.
Notice how he used movement to show the act of a kiss. In
Hopi Ceremonial Dance, Fred Kabotie chose another method
of showing movement to catch the act of the dance.
Although both artists have very different styles of painting,
they both tell a story through movement.

Fred Kabotie. (American). *Hopi Tashaf Kachina Dance.* 1936. Watercolor on paper. 18 × 22 inches. The Philbrook Museum of Art, Tulsa, Oklahoma.

Look at both paintings and notice the similarities and differences in the ways they show movement.

- ✓ Where do you see repeated lines, shapes, or objects in these paintings?

- ✓ How did the artists portray movement in their paintings?

- ✓ What clues do the artists give you in their paintings to tell you about their stories?

- ✓ Where are you in these stories? Are you an observer or a participant?

SEEING LIKE AN ARTIST

Think about a celebration you have participated in that was important to you. What one scene from that event would you want to illustrate?

Frozen and Progressive Motion

Illustrators can tell a story with a picture of an important event. Or they may draw a series of events to capture the action.

Frozen motion occurs when one action is "frozen" in time. Usually lots of images are in the artwork to tell the story.

Progressive motion occurs when a scene or motif changes a little each time it is repeated.

Practice

Draw a picture of an activity you have attended.

1. Divide a long, thin sheet of paper into six squares. Think of an activity at a celebration you have attended, such as blowing out candles at a birthday party.

2. Draw the activity in the first square exactly as you saw it. Then, change the scene slightly as you redraw it in each of the following squares until you reach an end, such as the candle going out, in the last square.

Decide Look at your illustrations. Can you see the event through your pictures only, or do you need words to explain them? Do you feel your work was successful?

Jennifer Flowers. Age 9. *A Day on the Swing.* Colored pencil and black felt-tip pen.

How does this student artist use rhythm?

Create

How can you use movement to illustrate your favorite story or song? Use visual movement to illustrate a story or song.

1. Think about the illustrations you have seen where movement showed feelings.

2. Choose a song, or story in which movement is important. Draw several sketches of its main events. Use rhythm to show visual movement.

3. Select the sketch that best illustrates the expressive quality of movement. Redraw it. Outline your drawing and fill it with color. Use repeated lines and shapes to create rhythm and movement.

Describe Describe the subject matter in your illustration.

Analyze How did you create the effect of visual movement in your illustration? Explain.

Interpret Was there a particular mood you wanted to create in your painting? If so, did you achieve it? If not, what mood did you create?

Decide Do you feel your illustration is successful? Why or why not? If you could go back and make some changes, what would they be?

Shapes, Rhythm, and Movement in Dance

Ballet Folklorico de Mexico:
"Danza de la Reata."

The folk dance in the picture is based on ranch life in Mexico. The male dancer twirls a lariat, or a rope that is used on ranches to rope cattle. At first he dances alone. Then he is joined inside the space of the twirling rope by a female dancer. The repeated shapes and curving lines of the rope and the dancers create a flowing rhythm.

70

What To Do

Create a dance based on a motion used in work.

Materials

✔ paper
✔ pencils

1. List different motions and objects people use in work, using a broom to sweep. Choose one to show in a dance.

2. Explore the rhythm involved in the motions of the work. For example, practice sweeping with an imaginary broom. Explore ideas for different ways that you can turn ordinary, sweeping motions into dance motion.

3. Share your ideas with a partner. Choose four of the best ideas, and work on them together. Practice your dance until you are comfortable.

4. Perform your dance. As you travel across the floor, you will create shapes and a flowing rhythm.

Describe Describe the shapes and movements that you and your partner created.

Analyze Explain how you created rhythm as you changed the work movement into a dance movement.

Interpret What moods did you create with fast or slow movements or flowing rhythm?

Decide Do you think you succeeded in changing work motions into dance motion?

Extra Credit

Choose some music to go with your dance. The music may influence your rhythm. Perform for an audience.

Wrapping Up **Unit 2**

Shape, Rhythm, and Movement

Reviewing Main Ideas

The lessons and activities in this unit are based on how artists use shape, rhythm, and movement in their artwork.

1. A **shape** is a flat or two-dimensional area that can be measured in only two ways: height and width. There are two basic types of shapes.

   • **Geometric** shapes, such as squares or triangles, can be made with a ruler or compass.

   • **Free-form** shapes are any shapes that are not geometric.

2. **Rhythm** is an art element created by repeating lines, shapes, or colors in a work of art. It is *visual* because you can see, but not hear it.

There are four types of rhythm.

   • **Random rhythm** has motifs in no apparent order and irregular spaces in between.

   • **Regular rhythm** has identical motif and equal spacing.

William H. Johnson. (American). *Sowing.* c. 1940. Oil on burlap. $38\frac{1}{2} \times 48\frac{3}{4}$ inches.

- **Alternating rhythm** has a motif that is changed in some way or a second motif is introduced.
- **Flowing rhythm** is created by repeating curved lines or shapes.

3. **Visual movement** is the illusion of motion or change in position. There are two types of visual movement.
   - **Frozen** — The movement or action is frozen in time much like a photograph.
   - **Progressive** — When a scene or object changes a little each time it is repeated.

Summing Up

Look at the painting by Johnson. He created figures using simplified shapes and repeated areas of color. They create rhythm and movement, which you learned about in this unit.

- Which shapes has Johnson repeated?
- Describe how Johnson created rhythm in his painting.
- Did Johnson use movement? If so, what type?

Shape, rhythm, and movement are important design principles that artists use to communicate to others what they see.

Careers in Art
Landscape Architect

David Barncord is a landscape architect. Landscape architects plan outdoor areas for people. They pay careful attention to protecting the environment. Barncord loved baseball as a boy, but there were no baseball fields near his home. He began laying out his own baseball fields when he was six years old. In his profession he works with architects, engineers, gardeners, building contractors, and various government officials. Barncord got his college degree in landscape architecture. He works long hours and meets many people in his work.

David Barncord, landscape architect

An Introduction to
Color and Value

Color is used by artists in paintings, drawings, and sculptures.

Miriam Shapiro. (Canadian). *Pas de Deux*. 1986. Acrylic and fabric on canvas. 90 × 96 inches. Collection: Dr. and Mrs. A. Acinapura/Courtesy Steinbaum Krauss Gallery, NYC.

Artists use *color* to create different moods and patterns.

- What colors do you see in *Pas de Deux*? Where do you see a bright color beside a dark color?
- What type of mood was created in this collage?
- Where are the neutral colors? The complementary colors on the woman's head and the background?

Artist Profile

Miriam Shapiro
1923–

Miriam Shapiro was born in 1923 in Toronto, Canada. She spent much of her childhood in the United States. In the 1950s she moved to New York to paint. She began working with patterned pieces of fabric, which she added to her paintings. She later added embroidered, appliquéd, and crocheted fabrics created by other women.

Miriam Shapiro and other artists use color to help communicate their ideas and feelings and as a way of bringing together the various parts of a work of art. In this unit you will learn and practice techniques using color. Here are the topics you will learn about:

- Color Spectrum
- Color Wheel
- Neutral Colors
- Complementary Colors
- Values: Tints and Shades
- Monochromatic Colors

The Color Wheel

Artists use the color wheel to organize colors
and understand how they work together.

David Hockney. (English). *Large Interior Los Angeles.* 1988. Oil, ink on cut and pasted paper on canvas.
Metropolitan Museum of Art, New York, New York. © David Hockney.

Both paintings on these pages use a wide range of color. David Hockney used a combination of bright primary colors with neutral colors in his painting. Stuart Davis used a mix of bright colors and unusual shapes. Notice how color is the most important element in both paintings.

Stuart Davis. (American). *Report from Rockport.* 1940. Oil on canvas. 24 × 30 inches. Metropolitan Museum of Art, NY, Edith and Milton Lowenthal Collection, Bequest of Edith Abrahamson Lowenthal, 1991.

Both artists use a variety of colors in their artwork.

✓ What colors did the artists use in their artworks?

✓ How did they separate colors in their artworks?

✓ Do the colors in each piece of art create the same feeling?

✓ If both artworks were done in only browns, blacks, and whites, would they communicate the same feelings and moods? Explain your answer.

SEEING LIKE AN ARTIST

Look around your classroom and notice how most objects have a dominant color.

The Color Spectrum

The colors in the **color spectrum**—red, orange, yellow, green, blue, and violet—appear in the same order in natural light. A rainbow is nature's color spectrum.

Red, yellow, and blue are the **primary colors**. You cannot mix any other colors to make them.

Secondary colors—orange, green, and violet—are created when two primary colors are mixed together. Primary and secondary colors are also called **hues**.

Intermediate colors are made by blending a primary color with a secondary color. Red-orange is an example of one of the six intermediate colors.

This **color wheel** is made up of three primary, three secondary, and six intermediate colors. Notice how the colors are organized so that you can easily understand how to mix a color.

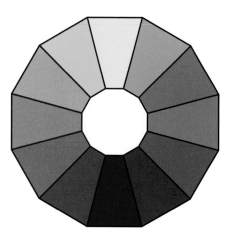

Practice

Create a geometric design. Use crayon.

1. Use a black marker to draw one large geometric shape touching at least two edges of a sheet of paper. Draw a second geometric shape inside your first shape, and then a third shape inside your second shape. Inside each section create geometric patterns.

2. Fill your design with color. In the center shape use primary colors. In the middle shape use secondary colors. In the outside shape use intermediate colors.

Decide Does your design have primary colors at the center, secondary colors in the middle, and intermediate colors in the outside? What changes would you make?

Amy Kus. Age 9. Mixed-media.

How did this student artist create a color wheel?

Create

What colors do you imagine you would see if you were a deep-sea diver in the Caribbean Sea? Create an undersea color-wheel drawing.

1. Imagine yourself swimming in the ocean. What creatures would you see?

2. Using pencil, draw a sea creature as large as your hand, adding details such as scales and teeth. Create an environment for your creature. Outline your drawing with black marker.

3. Divide your picture into 12 pie-shaped sections. Color each section as if it were part of a color wheel. Try to create as many of the colors as you can.

Describe What colors did you use in your drawing?

Analyze How did you create the intermediate colors in your drawing?

Interpret What would you choose as a title for your drawing?

Decide Were you successful in keeping your color wheel in sequenced order? Can you think of other themes that could be made into a color wheel?

Lesson 1

79

Neutral Colors

Neutral colors often create a quiet mood in a work of art.

Berthe Morisot. (French). *Woman at Her Toilette*. 1875. Oil on canvas. 60.3 × 80.4 cm.
Art Institute of Chicago, Chicago, Illinois/Stickney Fund, 1924. 127.

The painting by Berthe Morisot uses neutral colors with blues to create a quiet mood. Morisot often used much white in her bright scenes of domestic life. Ralph Steiner's black and white photograph has shades of gray, which add to the peaceful feeling. Both artists have used neutral colors in their pictures to help create a certain mood.

Ralph Steiner. (American). *American Rural Baroque.* 1930. Gelatin-silver print. 7 9/16 × 9 1/2 inches. The Museum of Modern Art, New York. Gift of the photographer. Copy print © 1998 The Museum of Modern Art, New York.

Both the painting and the photograph used neutral colors to express a feeling.

☑ What neutral colors are used in each of these pictures?

☑ Which color dominates in each picture? How does this color affect the overall mood of each picture?

☑ Describe the types of lines used in each picture. How do these lines add to the feeling of each picture?

☑ Look closely at both the painting and the photograph. How are they similar? How are they different?

Lesson 2

Using Neutral Colors

Black, white, and gray are **neutral colors**. They are often used to lighten or darken a color—to make it less bright—and to create a mood or feeling.

Mixing Neutral Colors When you add a neutral color to another hue or color, you change its **value**. This means you change the lightness or darkness of the color. Notice how the color below has been changed by adding neutral colors to it.

Practice

Draw a calm landscape using only neutral colors. Use crayons.

1. Create a landscape that looks peaceful and calm. On a sheet of paper, lightly sketch a simple landscape. Focus on simple shapes and do not worry about including details in your sketch.

2. Use crayons to color your landscape. Make sure that you use only neutral colors.

Decide How did you use neutral colors to create a calm feeling in your landscape? How would you use these colors to give your picture a nervous feeling? A feeling of mystery?

Yu Yoshio. Age 9. *My City*. Construction paper and oil pastel.

What mood did this student artist create?

Create

What colors would you use to describe a city's quiet mood? Use neutral colors of paper to create a collage of a city.

1. Think about the objects you see in a city. Make a rough sketch to plan your city scene. Use your sketch as a guide to create a collage.

2. Use black, white, or gray paper for your background. Cut a variety of shapes from papers that are neutral colors and contrast with your background. Fill the paper. Arrange your shapes before you glue them down.

3. Add details with neutral-colored oil pastels to create a mood in your picture.

Describe Describe the objects in your collage. What are some of the basic shapes you used to create your city scene?

Analyze How did you arrange shapes and colors to create a particular mood in your collage?

Interpret What mood did you create in your collage?

Decide Do you feel your city collage is successful? Explain.

Complementary Colors

Artists use complementary colors to create
contrast in their artworks.

Artist unknown. Tlingit (United States). *Yeihl Nax'in Raven Screen. c. 1830.* Spruce
and paint. $8\frac{13}{16} \times 10\frac{3}{4}$ feet. The Seattle Art Museum, Seattle, Washington, Gift of
John H. Haulberg. Photo by Paul Macapia.

The *Yeihl Nax'in Raven Screen* was made by a family
or clan from the Tlingit society. This partition was
used to block off a special room at the rear of the house.
The most valued clan possessions were kept behind it. The
tin canister was used to hold a variety of everyday items.
Both of these functional works of art have complementary
colors in their designs.

Artist unknown. (United States). *Canister.* 1825. Museum of American Folk Art, New York, New York.

Look closely at both works of art and talk about complementary colors.

- ✓ What are the main colors used in each artwork?

- ✓ How did the artists arrange these colors to create a design?

- ✓ What similarities and differences in the use of color do you see in these pieces of art?

- ✓ How do you feel when you look at both these works of art?

- ✓ What colors seem to show the greatest contrast in both works of art?

SEEING LIKE AN ARTIST

Think about your favorite color. Find a complementary color that looks best with it.

Using Complementary Colors

Colors that are opposite each other on the color wheel are **complementary colors**. For example, red is opposite green, so green is the complement of red. Complementary colors create **contrast**, or differences, in artwork. They make each other look very bright when used together.

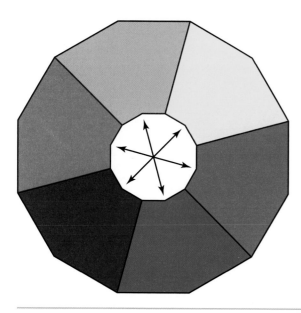

Notice that the complement of each primary color is a secondary color. What is the complement of blue or of yellow?

Complementary Sets Here are three sets of complementary colors. When used together, they can create exciting designs.

Practice

Create a design by experimenting with complementary colors. Use colored markers or crayons.

1. Sketch several simple designs on a sheet of paper using your initials. Choose one design and draw it three times on a second sheet of paper.

2. Color each design with one of the three sets of complementary colors. Use the color wheel as a guide.

Decide Look at your designs. Did you use three sets of complementary colors? Which do you prefer? Which do you like the least? Why?

Jenny Miller. Age 9. Cut paper.

What do you think this student artist's emblem stands for?

Create

What complementary colors would you use to design a school emblem? Use complementary colors to create a contrasting design.

1. Think about and list objects that best represent your school. Draw several simple shapes of the objects and select three.

2. Using paper the color of the primary colors, cut out the three shapes you selected. Glue each shape onto a square of paper that is the complementary color of the primary color.

3. Arrange the squares horizontally on a sheet of black paper. They can either touch or have spaces between them. Glue them in place.

Describe Describe the colors and shapes in your design.

Analyze Talk about how each shape represents an important thing about your school.

Interpret Discuss the emotion you were trying to present.

Decide Is your design successful in portraying your feelings about your school?

Low-Intensity Colors

Complementary colors can be used to dull a hue.

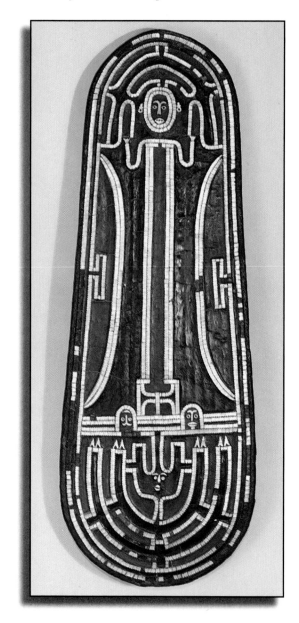

Artist unknown. Solomon Islands. c. 1852. *Ceremonial Shield* #59.63. Basketry, Nautilus shell inlay on resin base. $32\frac{1}{8} \times 9\frac{1}{4}$ inches. The Brooklyn Museum, Brooklyn, New York. Frank L. Babbott and Carll H. DeSilver Funds.

The *Ceremonial Shield* was woven from wicker on the Island of Guadalcanal and sold to the people of the Solomon Islands, who embellished it with small pieces of shell. On the other side of the world, Henri de Toulouse-Lautrec created the lithograph print *Le Jockey*. Both artworks are examples of the successful use of dull, low-intensity colors.

Henri de Toulouse-Lautrec. (French). *Le Jockey*. 1899.
Lithograph. $20\frac{1}{4} \times 14\frac{1}{8}$ inches. Collection of the
Brooklyn Museum, Brooklyn, New York.

Look at how colors are used in both these paintings.

- Name the colors you see in these paintings.
- What kind of colors are they?
- How does color affect the mood of each work?

SEEING LIKE AN ARTIST

Look around your room and notice where you find colors like those in the paintings.

Intensity

The brightness or dullness of a color is its **intensity**. For example, the yellow of a lemon is bright, therefore it is high in intensity. The yellow of mustard is much lower in intensity because it is a duller shade of yellow.

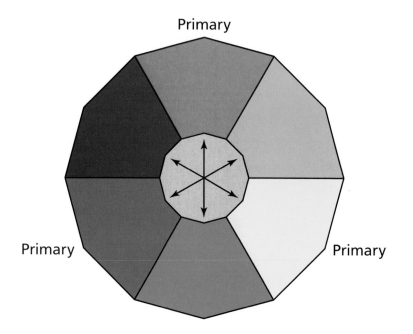

Mixing Complementary Colors When you mix a color with its complement, you lower its intensity; it becomes less bright. The more complementary color you add, the duller the color becomes. When you add equal amounts, you will create a brown or gray color.

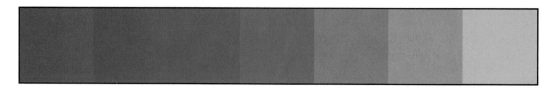

Practice

Experiment with intensity by mixing complementary colors. Use crayon.

1. Use one primary color, such as red, and color a light layer.

2. Color over the first color with its complement.

3. Try this again, using other sets of complements.

Decide How does mixing a complement affect the look of a primary color?

Cody Ellison. Age 9. *Rocky Desert*. Tempera.

If this student artist added animals to his landscape, what complementary colors could he use?

Create

What scenes come to mind when you think of a dull-colored or low-intensity landscape? Use complementary colors to create a low-intensity desert landscape.

1. Think about all the things you might find in a desert. What colors would they be?

2. Plan a desert landscape by drawing a few sketches. Include a variety of lines in your sketches.

3. Lightly draw your favorite sketch on a large piece of white paper. Begin by painting your background. Use complementary colors to create low-intensity colors for your desert landscape.

Describe Which set of complementary colors did you choose?

Analyze How did you create low-intensity colors? What problems did you have while painting and how did you solve them?

Interpret What mood do the colors in your painting create?

Decide Do you feel your painting was successful?

Tints and Shades of Complementary Colors

Artists make color lighter by adding white, and darker by adding black.

Emily Carr. (Canadian). *Sky*. 1936. Oil on canvas. 77.2 × 102.3 cm. National Gallery of Canada.

The paintings on these pages are by two artists whose uses of color are very similar. Notice how Emily Carr used value in her painting. *Niño con Paraguas,* which is Spanish for "Boy with a Parasol," was painted by Enrique Grau. Both artists used tints and shades to create light and dark values in their paintings.

Enrique Grau. (Colombian). *Niño con Paraguas.* 1964. Oil on canvas. 102 × 112 cm. Collection of the Art Museum of the Americas, Organization of American States.

Study both paintings and see how tints and shades are used.

☑ What are some of the colors used in both paintings?

☑ Are some colors darker or lighter than others? How did the artists create these colors?

☑ What are some similarities and differences in these paintings?

☑ How does the use of color help in creating a mood in these two paintings?

SEEING LIKE AN ARTIST
Look closely at a single object near you. Notice how that object reflects light. Now move the object. Are the lights and darks in the same area?

Lesson 5

Value of a Color

The **value** of a color is the darkness or lightness of that color. Light values are called **tints**. Dark values are called **shades**.

To create a **tint**, add white to a color. Tints are usually used to show areas where light touches the surface of the object drawn or painted. Tints are also used to show a sunny day and to create a feeling of happiness and joy.

To create a **shade**, add black to a color. Shades are used to show shadows and give the feeling of gloom and mystery to a work of art. Most artists do not use solid black for shadows; they use shades of color instead.

Practice

Create value scales by experimenting with tints and shades. Use tempera paints.

1. Fold a sheet of paper horizontally and open it up again. Label the top half "Tints" and the bottom half "Shades." Draw a long rectangle on each half and divide it into five sections.

2. Select a color for your tint. Add a drop or two of the color to white paint, and paint your first section. Add a drop or two more color each time you paint another section so that you have a gradual change from a very light tint to the pure color.

3. Use the same color for creating shades. Add black to your color to create shades of that color.

Decide Look at your value scales. Did you create a gradual change in value of tints and shades?

Jessica Flakes. Age 9. *Living Leaves*. Tempera.

How do you think this student artist created her tints and shades?

Create

What are some objects in nature that have one color with many different shades and tints? Use tints and shades to create a direct-observation painting.

1. Observe a plant, noting its basic shapes and contours. Lightly sketch the plant, making sure your drawing touches three edges of your paper.

2. Select a set of complementary colors. Using one color, paint your plant, adding black and white to create tints and shades of that color. Observe the shadows and highlights in the plant.

3. Paint the background with tints and shades of the second color.

Describe Describe the shapes and lines. Describe your complementary color scheme.

Analyze What did you notice when you were limited to only two colors plus black and white?

Interpret How does the value change affect the mood of your painting?

Decide Were you able to successfully produce a painting using tints and shades of complementary colors?

Lesson 5

Color Moods

Artists use colors to create moods.

Henri Rousseau. (French). *Carnival Evening.* 1886. Oil on canvas. $46 \times 35\frac{1}{4}$ inches. Philadelphia Museum of Art, Philadelphia, Pennsylvania. The Louis E. Stern Collection.

Both paintings on these pages show human figures, but our feelings about the people are strongly affected by their surroundings. Henri Rousseau surrounded two figures in party costumes with a mysterious forest. Yosa Buson isolates his traveler in a vast landscape. Both artists used colors to create moods.

Yosa Buson. (Japanese). *Landscape with a Solitary Traveler.* c. 1780. Hanging scroll. Ink and light colors on silk. 101.5 × 36.4 cm. Courtesy of the Kimbell Art Museum, Fort Worth, Texas.

Look at both paintings and notice the similarities and differences.

- What types of lines, shapes, and colors do you see? Are any of these elements repeated?

- How do you think the artists created the colors they used?

- Why do you think the artists chose the colors they used in their paintings?

- What feelings do you get when you look at these paintings?

SEEING LIKE AN ARTIST
Study an object with only one hue. What range of color values could you use to draw it? Make a line drawing of your object.

Lesson 6

Using Color Schemes

Monochromatic means "having one color."

This type of color scheme uses only one hue, or color, and the values of that color. For example, red, light red, and dark red, if used together without any other colors, would be considered a **monochromatic color scheme**.

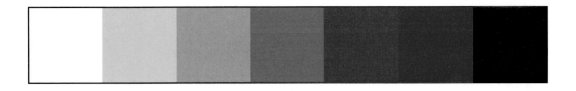

A **spectral color scheme** uses all six rainbow colors—red, orange, yellow, green, blue, and violet.

A **neutral color scheme** uses black, white, and a variety of grays.

A **complementary color scheme** uses one set of complementary colors, for example, red and green, blue and orange, and yellow and violet.

Practice

Design a watch using monochromatic colors. Use colored pencils and crayons.

Think of your favorite activity and design a watch using one crayon or one colored pencil along with black and white crayons or pencils. Use monochromatic colors to tie the design together.

Decide What effect did monochromatic colors have on your design? Did you use shapes to represent your favorite activity in your watch design?

Kelsey Fuller. Age 9. Tempera.

How would the feel of this artwork change if the student artist had used warm colors?

Create

What is your favorite color scheme? Select a color scheme to paint an imaginary scene that includes land, vegetation, buildings, and transportation.

1. Think about the way colors affect the look of a scene.

2. Make several sketches of an imaginary scene. Choose your best one.

3. Choose a color scheme that fits your scene. Fill your scene with color.

Describe Describe the things in your painting.

Analyze What color scheme did you use?

Interpret Was there a particular mood you wanted to create? If so, did you achieve it? Give it a poetic name.

Decide Do you feel that using a specific color scheme was helpful?

Color in Music

Bali and Beyond: Maria Bodmann and Cliff DeArment.

Painters work with a palette of colors. Composers of music work with a variety of sounds. Their "palette" is the wide range of sounds produced by voices, instruments, and the environment. For example, an artist might choose complementary colors to create a bright, exciting mood. A composer might choose harsh, clashing sounds to create an angry feeling. What sounds would create a happy feeling?

What To Do

Listen to the different sounds of different voices.

Materials

✔ cassette recorder

✔ a cassette tape of the voices of several adults who work in the school

1. Listen to the voices on the recording. See if you can identify the adults whose voices you hear. Notice that each voice has its own special sound.

2. Choose a song that has several verses and a chorus, such as "Clementine." Select different classmates to sing each verse. Have everyone join in on the chorus. Your teacher will record the song.

3. As the recording is played, listen for the special qualities of each solo voice. Discuss what makes each voice different in its "tone color" or sound quality.

Describe Describe two of the voices. Use adjectives such as *smooth, rough,* and *raspy*.

Analyze Explain how contrasting sounds are like complementary colors.

Interpret Tell how different tones of voices can create different feelings.

Decide How well were you able to identify the different "tone colors" or qualities of the voices?

Extra Credit

Listen to a recording of music that features two or three different instruments. Describe the "tone color" or sound quality of each instrument.

Color and Value

Reviewing Main Ideas

The lessons and activities in this unit cover techniques that artists use when creating color in their artwork.

1. A **color spectrum** has colors that appear in the **color wheel.**

2. **Primary colors** are red, yellow, and blue. No other colors can be mixed to make them.

3. **Secondary colors** are orange, green, and violet. They are created by mixing together two primary colors.

4. **Intermediate colors** are made when a primary color is mixed with a secondary color. (Red-orange)

5. A **color wheel** is made of the three primary, the three secondary, and six intermediate colors.

6. **Neutral colors** are black, white, and gray.

7. **Complementary colors** are opposite each other on the color wheel. (Red and green)

Robert Rauschenberg. (American). *Collection.* 1953–1954. Oil, paper, fabric and metal on wood. $80 \times 96 \times 3\frac{1}{2}$ inches. San Francisco Museum of Modern Art, Gift of Harry W. and Mary Margaret Anderson. Photo by Don Myer.

8. **Intensity** is the brightness or dullness of a color.

9. **Value** is the lightness or darkness of a color. There are two types of values.

   - A **tint** is created when a color is mixed with white to create a light value.

   - A **shade** is created when a color is mixed with black to create a dark value.

10. **Monochromatic** means "one color." This type of color scheme uses only one color and the values of that color. (blue, light blue, and dark blue)

Summing Up

American artist Robert Rauschenberg created the painting *Collection*. In this painting, Rauschenberg used the techniques in this unit to create color.

- What are some of the colors you see in Rauschenberg's painting? What color did he use most often?

- Did Rauschenberg use any of the color schemes you learned about in this unit? Explain your answer.

- Do you see any values? Describe them.

Color is an important art element in painting, drawing, and sculpture. Artists use color to suggest a feeling and to express an idea.

Let's Visit a Museum

The San Francisco Museum of Modern Art in California was the first museum on the West Coast built to hold only twentieth-century art. The museum has more than 15,000 works of art in its collection. The collection consists of modern and contemporary art including paintings, sculptures, photographs, architectural drawings, and models. The museum is also known for its wide collection of art from California artists. In addition to the exhibits, the museum offers lectures, special events, and many activities for seniors and children.

The San Francisco Museum of Modern Art

An Introduction to
Form

Artists use form to create three-dimensional works of art.

Henry Moore. (American). *Reclining Mother and Child*. 1960–1961. Bronze. 90 × 35½ × 52 inches. Collection Walker Art Center, Minneapolis, Minnesota. Gift of Frederick R. Weisman in honor of his parents, William and Mary Weisman, 1988.

Artists use different types of **forms** to communicate their feelings and ideas and to show how they see the world. They also create forms for use in daily life.

- What is the difference between this sculpture and a drawing?
- Describe the open and solid areas of the sculpture. What basic shape do you see?
- Point out the mother and child in this sculpture. What did Henry Moore do to the figures? Why do you think he did this?
- From how many sides would you view this sculpture? Do you think Moore intended his viewers to observe this sculpture from many angles? Explain why.

Artist Profile

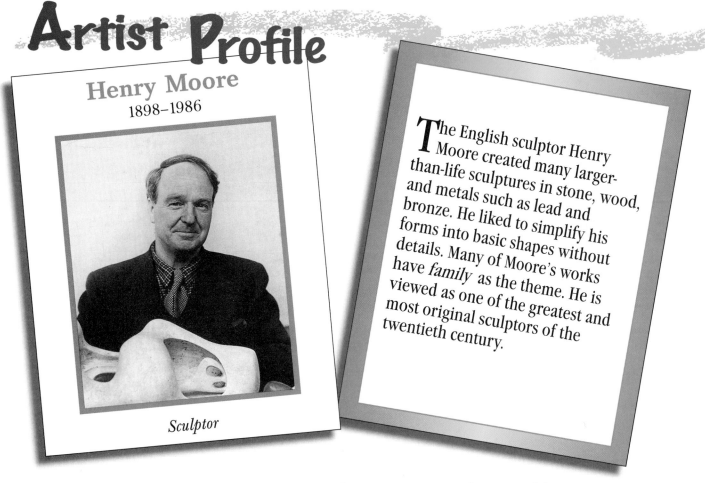

Henry Moore
1898–1986

Sculptor

The English sculptor Henry Moore created many larger-than-life sculptures in stone, wood, and metals such as lead and bronze. He liked to simplify his forms into basic shapes without details. Many of Moore's works have *family* as the theme. He is viewed as one of the greatest and most original sculptors of the twentieth century.

Henry Moore and other sculptors use form to communicate an idea or to create a useful object. In this unit you will learn about using form to express ideas and to understand different ways that artists create forms. Here are the topics you will study.

- Forms
- Additive Sculpture
- Subtractive Sculpture
- Masks
- Functional Forms
- Assembled Forms

105

Forms

Sculptors communicate their feelings, ideas, and views of the world through form.

Henry Moore. (English). *Family Group.* 1948–50. Bronze. $59\frac{1}{4} \times 46\frac{1}{2} \times 29\frac{7}{8}$ inches. The Museum of Modern Art, New York, New York. A Conger Goodyear Fund. Photograph © 1988.

The sculptures on these pages represent people. Henry Moore used rounded forms in *Family Group,* a larger-than-life sculpture. Twenty years earlier, Jacques Lipchitz carved the 16-inch marble statue *Reclining Figure.* He used simple, flat forms. Both artists communicated through forms.

Jacques Lipchitz. *Reclining Figure with Guitar.* 1928. Black marble. $16\frac{3}{8} \times 27\frac{5}{8} \times 13\frac{1}{2}$ inches. © 1998 Estate of Jacques Lipchitz/Licensed by Vaga, New York, NY, Marlborough Gallery, New York, The Museum of Modern Art, New York, New York. Mrs. John D. Rockefeller 3rd Bequest, Photograph © 1998.

Study the two sculptures to see how the artists worked with form.

✓ What kinds of forms do you see in each sculpture?

✓ List the similarities and differences in the look of each work.

✓ Do the types of lines used in each sculpture communicate a certain feeling?

✓ What are the figures doing?

✓ Why do you think the artists chose to make their sculptures abstract rather than realistic?

SEEING LIKE AN ARTIST

Look around you. Notice the many objects that have three or more surfaces, like your desk, your pencil, and even this book.

Lesson 1

Using Forms and Shapes

A **shape**, such as a square, is **two dimensional**. It is flat and can be measured only two ways: by length and by width.

A **form**, such as a cube or sphere, is **three dimensional**. It can be measured in three ways: by its length, width, and depth. Think of a form as a solid object that has thickness. You can see in the following illustration how shapes and forms are related.

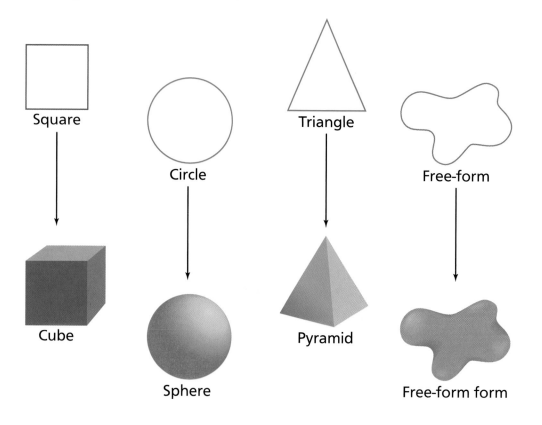

Square

Circle

Triangle

Free-form

Cube

Sphere

Pyramid

Free-form form

Practice

Change shapes into forms. Use colored pencils.

1. Draw a shape, two times. Color each shape a solid color.

2. Change the second shape into a form, creating the illusion of three dimensions by adding more lines and shading. Blend complementary colors together for shadows.

Analyze Were you able to successfully change a shape to a form? What techniques did you find helpful in doing this?

Is this student artwork free-form or geometric?

Ellen Jacobs. Age 9. *Creation*. Clay.

Create

What forms would you choose to create? Use clay to model a sculptured form that is interesting from every point of view.

1. Think about the different forms you see every day. Some are natural, organic forms, and some are made by people.

2. Form a large potato shape out of clay. Keep turning your form, making sure to work on all surfaces. Use your fingers to press into the surface and to pull up other surfaces. Create at least one curved hole that goes completely through the clay.

Describe Describe the form you have created. Explain how you made your form.

Analyze How did you turn a basic shape into a form? Did you use free-form or geometric forms?

Interpret What does your work look like?

Decide Is your form interesting from every point of view?

Additive Sculpture

Adding something to a sculpture is one technique for changing a form.

Artist unknown. (Peru). *Church Quinua.* From the Girard Foundation Collection, in the Museum of Internatonal Folk Art, a unit of the Museum of New Mexico, Santa Fe, NM. Photographer: Michel Monteau.

Both the clay forms on these pages are folk art. The artists who created them did not have formal art training. *Church Quinua* is typical of the clay work from Peru. *Woman,* by Teodora Blanco, was made in Mexico. Notice how both forms look more interesting because of the addition of clay to their surface.

Teodora Blanco. (Mexican).
Woman, c. 1965.

Study both sculptures to see how the artists used decorative techniques.

✓ What kinds of forms were used to create each sculpture?

✓ Describe the forms that were added to each sculpture.

✓ Which is an example of free-form and which is geometric?

SEEING LIKE AN ARTIST

Think about the buildings in your neighborhood. Which ones have decorative forms added to their surfaces to make them interesting?

Creating Additive Sculpture

Sculpture is any three-dimensional piece of art. One type of sculpture in which objects stick out from a flat surface is **relief sculpture**. Another type, **freestanding sculpture**, is surrounded by space on all sides.

When something is added to either relief or freestanding sculpture, it becomes an **additive sculpture**. Materials such as paper, cardboard, metal, and wood can be used to create additive sculptures.

Practice

Build a temporary additive relief sculpture. Use items found in your desk.

Create an additive relief sculpture on your desk using only items found in your desk. Use a variety of shapes and sizes. Place items such as erasers, rulers, and books carefully to make your sculpture interesting.

Describe What did you use to build your sculpture? What types of forms did you use in your sculpture?

What geometric shapes are on this student artist's building front?

Molly B. Age 9. *Building Front*. Clay and paint.

Create

How would you redesign the front of your favorite building? Create a relief design for the front of the building using additive sculpture.

1. Think about the house and storefronts you pass every day in your environment. Make several sketches to plan the front of your building.

2. Use a thick slab of clay to form the base of your sculpture. Add windows, doors, signs, and other details.

Describe Explain how you created your relief sculpture.

Analyze Describe the forms you added to your clay slab. Did you add both free-form and geometric forms?

Interpret Talk about the function of your building. Is it a home for a particular person or the front of a public building?

Decide What could you do differently to change the feeling of the sculpture?

Subtractive Sculpture

Artists carve into a form to alter its appearance so that an idea can be expressed.

Artist unknown. Aztec (Mexico). *Jaguar.* Stone. 12.5 × 14.5 × 28 cm. 1440–1852. The Brooklyn Museum. 38.45 Carll H. DeSilver Fund.

Look at the artwork on these pages. Both forms are simple, without any additive detail. The Aztec *Jaguar* was carved from stone more than 400 years ago. *Egyptian Cat* was made around 950–300 B.C. Notice that although both are carved cat sculptures, they look very different.

Artist unknown. (Egypt). *Egyptian Cat.* Late Dynastic Bronze. 12 × 7.6 cm.
The Metropolitan Museum of Art, New York, New York. Purchase, 1966, Fletcher
Fund and the Guide Foundation, Inc. gift.

Compare the two works of art.

✓ What kinds of forms have the artists used?

✓ What are some similarities and differences in these
   sculptures?

✓ Which sculpture has open areas? How does this affect
   its look?

✓ How did the artists show the unique characteristics of
   these animals?

**SEEING LIKE
AN ARTIST**
What is your favorite
animal? Think about
all the qualities that
make that animal
unique.

Lesson 3

Using Positive and Negative Space

Artists can change a form by carving. When an artist carves away from a form, it is called **subtractive sculpture**. This is because part of the original material is being taken away or subtracted.

The figure, shape, or object is the **positive space**. It takes up room and is usually the first thing we notice when looking at a work of art.

Some forms are created so that we can move around them and see them from all sides. The area around, under, above, and between objects is the **negative space**. It is the area or "air" around the object.

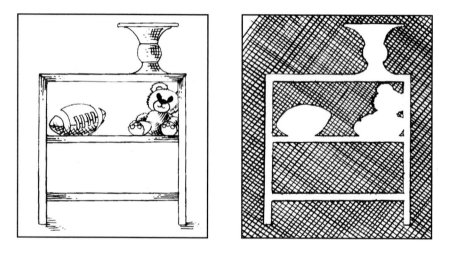

Notice how the negative space can be as important as the form itself.

Practice

Experiment using positive and negative space in a sculpture design. Use pencil.

1. Draw a square or rectangle. Using the side of the pencil point, color the shape evenly. Do not bear down with the point.

2. Think of a design you would like to create. Using an eraser, carefully subtract the negative spaces and watch your sculpture design appear.

Decide Do you see the importance of positive and negative space? Do you see any changes you need to make in your design?

Benny Kosto. Age 9. *The White Dog*. Soap.

Where is the negative space in this carving?

Create

What simple animal form would you choose to carve? Carve an animal out of plaster or a bar of soap.

1. Think of animals that live in your environment and those that live in the wild. Make a simplified drawing of one animal.

2. Draw the basic shape of your animal onto the plaster or the soap bar. Slowly begin to carve off small pieces using a spoon, paper clip, or strong plastic knife.

3. Keep turning your form so that you are working on all surfaces equally. You cannot add to it, so work slowly.

Describe Describe the animal you created.

Analyze What kind of form did you carve? Did you include negative space?

Interpret Give your sculpture a name.

Decide Were you successful in carving your animal?

Forms in Masks

Artists make masks for many reasons.

Artist unknown. (New Guinea). *Turtle Shell Mask.* Turtle shell, clam shell, wood, sennit paint, fiber, resin, and feathers. 17$\frac{1}{2}$ inches. Metropolitan Museum of Art, New York, New York.

The two masks on these pages were made in different areas of the world. The *Turtle Shell Mask* from New Guinea is an exciting mask with many different parts to catch your eye. The *Face Mask* from the Ivory Coast of Africa is the carved wooden face of a woman. What kind of ceremony do you think each mask was used for?

Artist unknown. Baule. (Ivory Coast). *Face Mask.*
Wood. $8\frac{1}{2}$ inches. Metropolitan Museum.

Look at the two masks and study all their parts.

☑ What shapes and patterns do you see?

☑ How is the feeling of one mask different from the other? What gives each mask its special feeling?

☑ What do you think was the purpose of each mask?

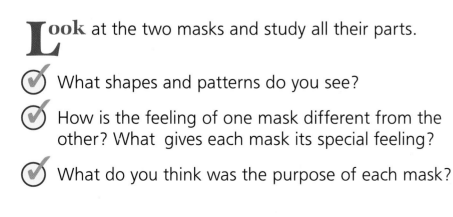

SEEING LIKE AN ARTIST

Masks have been used in various cultures for centuries. Think about all the various modern-day masks that we use in our culture and the reasons we use them.

Lesson 4

Using Proportions

Artists use **proportion** to make things look real or lifelike. Things appear to be the right size. Most people like artwork that is in proportion because it is easy to recognize and understand. Artists will often take exact measurements when making a work of art in proportion.

Artists will sometimes use **distortion** to exaggerate an object. This involves stretching, bending, twisting, or changing the sizes of objects from their normal proportions. Distortion is often used to communicate an idea or strong emotion. Enlarged eyes, for example, could suggest fear or wonder. Distorted forms can be found in many different kinds of art.

Practice

Draw a proportioned face. Use pencil.

1. Work with a partner. Have your partner make a face expressing a strong emotion. Sketch the face emphasizing the emotion.

2. Your classmate can then sketch your face showing a strong emotion.

Decide Study your drawing. Have you captured the emotion?

Wandale Gore. Age 9. *Leopard Mask*. Papier-Mâché and tempera.

How would you describe this student artist's mask?

Create

What emotion would you like to show in a mask? Create a papier-mâché mask that exaggerates the emotion you want to show.

1. Think about your face. Draw several sketches, each showing a different emotion.

2. Create a mold using one of your sketches. Cover it with papier-mâché.

3. Paint your mask when it is completely dry. Complete your mask by decorating it with other colors of paint and various materials.

Describe What shapes and forms did you use in your mask?

Analyze How did you use proportion or distortion in your mask?

Interpret What emotion does your mask represent?

Decide Do you feel your mask was successful in showing the emotion you chose? What would you do to improve it?

Functional Forms

Functional forms are made by artists for use in daily life.

Artist unknown. (China). *Model of a house.* Eastern Han Dynasty, A.D. 25-220. Glazed tomb pottery. $41 \times 22\frac{5}{8}$ inches. Metropolitan Museum of Art, New York, New York. Purchase, Dr. and Mrs. John C. Weber gift, 1984.

Look at the clay architectural buildings on these pages. The model of a grain tower was made between A.D. 221–227 in the western region of the Han Dynasty. Earlier, the model of a house was made in China's eastern region. It is an example of the type of houses people lived in there. Models like the ones on these two pages were placed in tombs.

Artist unknown. (China). *Grain Tower.* Chinese Three Kingdoms Period, A.D. 221–227 Pottery, grey clay. Om 216. Philadelphia Museum of Art, The Dr. George Crofts Collection, Given by Charles H. Ludington, Philadelphia, Pennsylvania.

Observe how both architectural models were formed.

☑ What shapes were used to create these clay forms?

☑ Discuss the positive and negative spaces. How did the artists create them?

☑ What are similarities and differences in the models?

☑ What function or purpose do you think they served?

☑ Could they be used as containers? What might they hold?

SEEING LIKE AN ARTIST

Look around your room. Find objects that are functional or serve a purpose.

Creating Functional Forms

Functional forms are objects created by artists for use in daily life. Sometimes they have decorative surfaces and other times the surfaces are very simple. One type of functional form is a container, such as a jar or bottle.

The form of a container is the **positive space**. This is the part that we can see and touch. The inside of a container has **negative space**. This space is taken up by what the container holds.

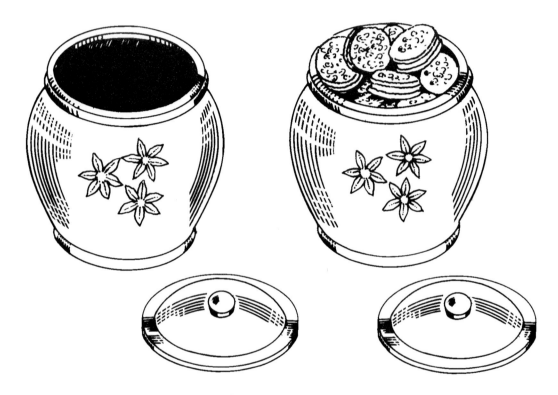

Practice

Look for functional containers in your classroom.

List the forms in your classroom that are the functional containers. Separate your list into two sections—free-form and geometric.

Decide Look at your list. Are there more free-form or more geometric containers in the room?

What might this student artist keep in his container?

Ramon Bonilla. Age 9. *Hidden Stuff.* Clay and paint.

Create

What treasure do you have that you would like to keep in a special container? Create a functional container to hold your special treasure.

1. Think about the form of the container you will need to hold your treasure.

2. Draw several sketches of a container. Select the one that you like best.

3. Use slabs and coils to build your clay container with a removable lid.

4. Decorate your finished container by pressing in textures, adding clay details, and drawing patterns into the surface.

Describe Describe the form of your container. What textures and patterns did you create on the surfaces?

Analyze Is the negative space large enough to hold your treasure?

Interpret Explain the function of your container.

Decide Were you able to successfully produce a container using the slab and coil methods?

Assembled Forms

Artists combine a variety of materials to create an assemblage.

Simon Rodia. (Italian). *Watts Towers.* 1921–59. Concrete. Los Angeles, California.

Look at both these works of art. Simon Rodia collected broken tiles, glass, and other objects he found and embedded them into concrete to make *Watts Towers.* This famous folk art structure took 33 years to complete. Artist Jane Rhoades Hudak made her handmade paper interesting by adding found objects to her wet paper pulp.

Jane Rhoades Hudak. (American). Handmade paper. Private collection.

Study the materials used in both works of art.

- ✓ Find an unusual art material in each form.
- ✓ Describe the materials used in both works.
- ✓ What did the artists use as their base materials?
- ✓ Why do you think the artists created these works?

Seeing Like an Artist

Look around for things that you could add to a piece of art.

Creating an Assemblage Form

An **assemblage** is a technique in which an artist collects found materials and assembles them to create a work of art that expresses an idea or feeling. **Found materials** are any items found in your home, school, or outdoor environment that can be used to create new works of art.

There are two different kinds of assemblages. A **relief assemblage** has objects that stick out from one side only. A **freestanding assemblage** has space all around it and is meant to be seen from all sides.

A handmade paper assemblage is an example of a relief assemblage. Found materials can be added to it at two stages. They can be pressed into wet pulp after the paper has been removed from a **deckle**, a framed screen used for papermaking. Materials can also be added onto the paper when it dries.

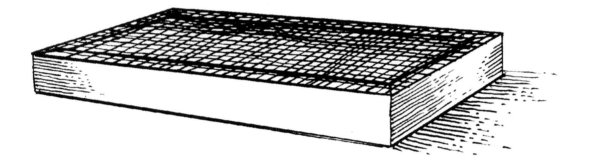

Practice

Practice making paper pulp. Use a variety of paper scraps.

1. Collect a variety of different types of paper. Scraps will work fine.

2. In small groups, experiment to see which types of paper make pulp that sticks together best. Do this by adding water to each type of collected paper and squeezing the pulp with your fingers.

Decide Which recycled paper will make the best pulp?

Suna Sung. Age 9. Paper pulp and yarn.

Name three more found objects that could be
added to this assemblage.

Create

**How can you use recycled materials to
make a paper assemblage? Use a variety of
materials in creating your assemblage.**

1. Think about things you can add to your wet
   paper pulp and things that could be glued
   onto the paper when it is dry.

2. Make paper pulp and add some of your found
   materials. Press and shape the pulp.

3. Spread the remainder of your materials out
   before you. Arrange and rearrange objects you
   think might go together. Glue them onto the
   dried paper.

Describe Describe the items you
chose for your handmade paper
assemblage.

Analyze Explain why you chose
the objects contained in and on
your assemblage.

Interpret Give your paper
assemblage a title.

Decide Were you successful in
using recycled materials to create
something new?

Forms in Pantomime

The Chameleons: Sharon Diskin and Keith Berger.

mime partners take on the role of characters involved in real-life situations. They do this through body language, facial expressions, and gestures. They communicate feelings and ideas by adjusting their body shapes and postures. They change the forms of their bodies to express different emotions.

What To Do

Mime the roles of a sculptor and the stone that is sculpted.

Materials

None

1. Work with a partner. Partner A will take the role of a sculptor. Partner B will take the role of a "cooperative" stone that is being sculpted.

2. The sculptor uses an imaginary mallet and chisel to carve the stone. The stone shows the changes in shape and form that occur as the sculptor works.

3. The sculptor makes a few movements. Then the sculptor waits to give the stone time to alter his or her shape.

4. When finished, the sculptor may walk around the work and choose a title for it.

5. Switch roles with your partner.

Describe How did you create the role of sculptor and the role of the stone?

Analyze Explain how you used forms to communicate ideas.

Interpret Tell what feelings your "sculpture" expressed.

Decide How well did you succeed in miming the characters? What would you do differently another time?

Extra Credit

Create a new sculpture. Then have partner B move in slow motion from the final sculpted form to a new form, and then back to the original form.

Form

Reviewing Main Ideas

The lessons and activities in this unit are based on how artists use form to create sculptures and containers.

1. A **shape** is two-dimensional and can be measured by length and width.

2. A **form** is a three-dimensional object that can be measured in three ways: length, height, and width. Examples are the cube, sphere, pyramid, and free-form.

3. A **sculpture** is a three-dimensional work of art that can be created out of wood, stone, metal, paper, or clay. There are two terms to describe the way a sculpture has been made.

There are two types of sculpture.

- **Relief** sculpture has objects sticking out from a flat surface.
- **Freestanding** sculpture is surrounded by space on all sides.

4. **Additive sculpture** has objects added to the base or main form.

5. **Subtractive sculpture** is created by carving away from a form.

6. **Positive space** is the figure or form in three-dimensional art.

Henry Moore. (British). *Knife Edge Mirror Two Pieces.* 1977–1978. Bronze. 210½ × 284 × 143 inches. National Gallery of Art, Washington, DC. Gift of the Morris and Gwendolyn Cafritz Foundation.

7. **Negative space** is the area around, under, above, and between objects.

8. **Proportion** occurs when things look real or lifelike.

9. **Distortion** involves exaggerating a figure, object, or feature.

10. A **functional form** is an item made by an artist for use in daily life, such as a bowl.

11. An **assemblage** is a sculpting technique in which a variety of materials is assembled to create a work of art.

Summing Up

Look at the sculpture by Moore. Notice that he used some of the techniques that you learned about in this unit.

• Why is *Knife Edge Mirror Two Piece* considered a three-dimensional form?

• Is this sculpture an example of additive or subtractive sculpture? Is it a relief sculpture? Why or why not?

• Describe the negative and positive spaces. What shapes and forms do they remind you of?

Form is important to artists because they use it to create art in three dimensions. Artists use form to create decorative and functional works of art.

Careers in Art
Museum Director

J. Carter Brown is Director Emeritus of the National Gallery of Art in Washington, DC. He was the director from 1969 to 1992. After his retirement, he collected 129 works of art from 39 countries for an exhibition that was part of the 1996 Olympic Arts Festival in Atlanta, Georgia. From the time he was quite young, Brown knew that he wanted a career in the arts; he just wasn't quite sure what it would be. A museum director came to his university to give a speech and from then on, he knew what he wanted to do. He prepared in many ways, one of which was studying art history.

J. Carter Brown

An Introduction to
Space and Texture

Artists create space and texture in paintings
to show how things look and feel.

Vincent van Gogh. (Dutch). *The Starry Night.* 1889. Oil on canvas. $28\frac{3}{4} \times 36\frac{1}{2}$ inches.
The Museum of Modern Art, New York, New York. Acquired through the Lillie P. Bliss bequest.

Artists create **space** in paintings to give the appearance of depth on a flat surface.

- How do you think Vincent van Gogh created space in *The Starry Night?*

- Which objects in the painting look closer to you? Which objects look farther away?

Artists create **texture** in paintings to show how things might feel if you touch them.

- How would you describe the texture of the sky? The buildings?

Artist **P**rofile

Vincent van Gogh
1853–1890

Self-Portrait with a Straw Hat.

Vincent van Gogh was born March 30, 1853, in a small village in Holland. He decided to express human emotion and feelings through art. Only after failed attempts at becoming a missionary and an art dealer. He is best known for using bright colors and active brush strokes. During the last ten years of his life, van Gogh made over 1,600 paintings and drawings. His work has made an impact on the art world that is recognized today.

Vincent van Gogh and other artists use space and texture to show how things look and feel. In this unit you will learn and practice the techniques that artists use to create space and texture in their paintings. Here are the topics you will study:

- Perspective
- Point of View
- Tactile Texture
- Visual Texture

Perspective

Artists use perspective techniques in paintings to make things seem close or far away.

Grant Wood. (American). *The Birthplace of Herbert Hoover, West Branch, Iowa.* 1931. Oil on composition board. $29\frac{5}{8} \times 39\frac{3}{4}$ inches. The Minneapolis Institute of Arts, Minneapolis, Minnesota. © 1998 Estate of Grant Wood/Licensed by VAGA, New York, NY.

Look at the paintings on these pages. *The Birthplace of Herbert Hoover* was painted by Grant Wood in the Midwest region of the United States. *The Bicycle Race* was painted by Antonio Ruiz at about the same time in Mexico. Both artists have used perspective techniques to create the illusion of depth in their pictures.

Antonio Ruiz. (Mexican). *The Bicycle Race.* 1938. Oil on canvas. $14\frac{1}{2} \times 16\frac{1}{2}$ inches. Phildelphia Museum of Art, Philadelphia, Pennsylvania. Purchased by Nebinger Fund.

Study both paintings to find examples of perspective techniques.

✓ Find an object that overlaps and covers part of a second object.

✓ Find an object that seems to be close to you. Find an object that seems to be far away.

✓ Find objects with very clear details. Find objects with few details.

✓ Find objects that are painted with bright colors. Find objects that are painted with dull colors.

✓ Find lines that seem to be getting closer together as they move away from you.

SEEING LIKE AN ARTIST

Look across your classroom. Find objects and lines like the ones you found in the paintings.

Lesson 1

Using Perspective

Perspective is the technique used to create the feeling of depth on a flat surface. **Depth** is the appearance of distance on a flat surface. You saw examples of the following six perspective techniques in the two paintings on the previous pages.

Overlapping When one object covers part of a second object, the first seems to be closer to the viewer.

Size Large objects seem to be closer to the viewer than small objects.

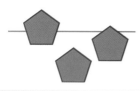

Placement Objects placed near the bottom of a picture seem to be closer to the viewer than objects placed higher on the picture.

Detail Objects with clear, sharp edges and many details seem to be closer to the viewer. Objects that lack detail and have fuzzy outlines seem to be farther away.

Lines Parallel lines seem to move toward the same point as they move farther away from the viewer.

Color Brightly colored objects seem closer to the viewer. Objects with pale, dull colors seem to be farther away.

Practice

Illustrate each of the six perspective techniques. Use pencil.

1. Fold your paper into six equal boxes. Print the name of one perspective technique in the upper-left corner of each of the six boxes.

2. Draw designs to illustrate each perspective technique.

Decide Have you drawn all of your examples correctly? Which ones do you need to change? How would you change them to make them correct?

Casie Young. Age 9. *Winter Wonderland.* Tempera.

How did this student artist create a feeling of depth in a landscape?

Create

How can a landscape show perspective? Use perspective techniques in a landscape scene.

1. Think about the things you see in your environment every day.

2. Sketch several scenes you would like to draw. Include all six perspective techniques in your sketches.

3. Select your best sketch. Use chalk to draw the scene, and fill it with color. Remember to use all six perspective techniques that create the feeling of depth.

Describe Describe the subject matter of your painting.

Analyze How did you use perspective techniques to create the illusion of depth in your painting?

Interpret What kind of mood have you created in your painting? Which element do you think affects this mood most?

Decide If you could redo this painting, what would you do to improve it?

Environmental Perspective

Some artists use high and low placement to create the illusion of depth.

Joaquin Torres-Garcia. (Uruguayan). *Bird's Eye View.* Gouache and watercolor on board. $13\frac{1}{4} \times 19\frac{1}{8}$ inches. Yale University Art Gallery.

The paintings on these two pages show depth. Artist Joaquin Torres-Garcia traveled to many countries. His two-year visit to New York City greatly influenced his work. Carmen Lomas Garza's art illustrates everyday events in her Texas community. Both artists use high and low placement to show depth in their paintings.

Carmen Lomas Garza. (American). *Cakewalk*. 1987. Acrylics. 36 × 48 inches. Collection of Paula Maciel-Benecke and Norbert Benecke, Soquel, California. Photo by M. Lee Fatherree.

Study both paintings to discover the artists' use of placement and size to show depth.

✓ Where do you see change in size?

✓ What objects appear closer to the viewer?

✓ What objects appear farthest away from the viewer?

SEEING LIKE AN ARTIST

Point down at your shoe and then look at a friend's shoe far away. Does one shoe seem larger than the other?

Lesson 2

Using Perspective to Create the Illusion of Depth

A **picture plane** is the surface of a drawing or painting. There are three terms used to describe the high and low placement of objects on a picture plane—foreground, middle ground, and background.

The **foreground** is the part of the picture plane that appears closest to the viewer. The foreground is usually at the bottom of the picture plane.

The **background** is the part of the picture plane that seems to be farthest from the viewer. It is usually located at the top of the picture plane.

The **middle ground** is the area in a picture between the foreground and background.

Practice

Play "Perspective Jeopardy." Use landscape pictures.

Work in small groups. One person in the group names an object in the landscape. Another person in the group tells whether the object is in the foreground, middle ground, or background.

Decide Which area in the landscape was hardest to identify?

Megan Riley. Age 9. Charcoal.

What did this student artist draw in the foreground, the background, and the middle ground?

Create

What in your environment could you use to make an interesting perspective drawing? Use perspective techniques.

1. Think about details in your environment that you might include in your drawing.

2. Look through a viewing frame, and do two quick sketches of different areas. Choose one to make into a finished drawing.

3. Divide the picture plane on your paper into foreground, background, and middle ground. Begin by drawing the larger shapes of the foreground. Then, fill in the middle ground and next the background. Finish by adding details to your foreground.

Describe Describe the scene you drew. Where on the picture plane are your shapes and objects?

Analyze Explain how you used foreground, background, and middle ground. How did you create the illusion of depth?

Interpret Give your work a creative title.

Decide Do you feel you were successful in creating the illusion of depth? Explain.

Perspective Murals

Some artists make murals that show deep space.

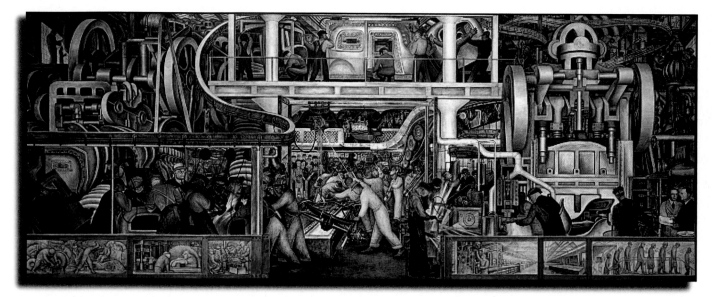

Diego M. Rivera. (Mexican). *Detroit Industry, South Wall.* 1932–33. Fresco. The Detroit Institute of Arts, Detroit, Michigan. Photograph © 1996. Gift of Edsel B. Ford.

Look at the mural and its detail on these two pages. Diego Rivera painted many murals in Mexico and in the United States. This mural depicts the Detroit auto industry and the people who worked in it in the 1930s. Notice how deep space is shown in the detail.

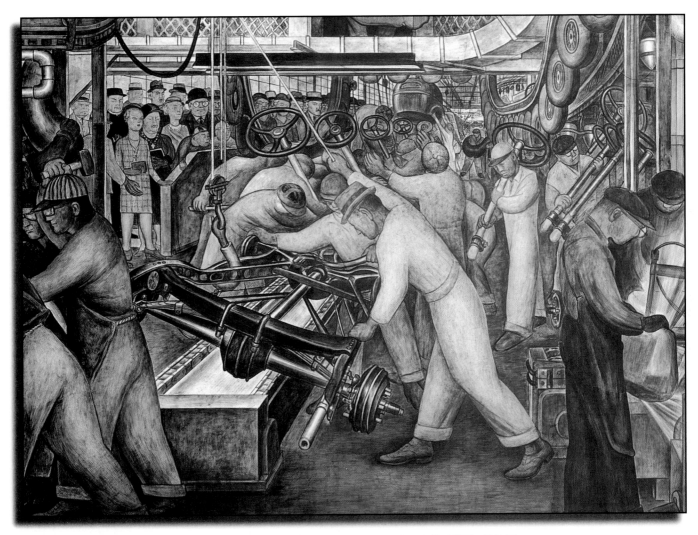

Diego M. Rivera. (Mexican). *Detail of Detroit Industry, South Wall.* 1932–33. Fresco. The Detroit Institute of Arts, Detroit, Michigan. Photograph © 1996. Gift of Edsel B. Ford.

Study the mural and its detail to find the following perspective techniques that create the illusion of depth.

☑ What objects or people appear closest to the viewer?

☑ What objects or people appear farthest away from the viewer?

☑ What is the setting of Rivera's mural? Does this place appear to be large or small? Why?

SEEING LIKE AN ARTIST

Hold out your hand in front of you. Close one eye and look at your hand. Then look past your hand. Compare the size of your hand to the objects that are farthest away.

Using Perspective to Create a Mural

A **mural** is a large piece of art painted on a wall. Some artists create murals that have **perspective**. These murals create the feeling of deep space.

There are six **perspective techniques**—overlapping, size variation, high and low placement, detail, converging lines, and color. Together, these techniques create the feeling of depth on a flat surface.

Practice

1. Look across the room at a particular object. Hold up a pencil to measure the object's height by sight.

2. Then, walk over to the object and measure it with your pencil again.

3. Measure a couple other objects in this way.

Decide Explain the difference in sizes.

Carla Delgado. Age 9. *Having Fun.* Tempera.

Where could you display this student artist's mural in your school?

Create

What deep space scene could be used to create an interesting mural in your school? Design a mural that creates the illusion of depth.

1. Think about murals you have seen—where they have been displayed and what themes were used. Working in small groups, discuss a theme for a mural.

2. Make several sketches applying perspective techniques to illustrate the illusion of depth.

3. Select the best sketch and draw a proposal for a mural. Paint your drawing.

Describe Describe your theme and the objects, shapes, and lines used in your mural design.

Analyze Describe how you used perspective techniques in your mural design to create the illusion of depth.

Interpret What feeling did you create in your design? What title might you give it?

Decide Were you able to successfully plan a mural using perspective techniques to illustrate the illusion of depth?

Point of View

Artists often study an object or scene from different points of view.

Michael Naranjo. Santa Clara Pueblo (American). *Eagle's Song.* Bronze.
Photography by © 1995 Mark Nohl.

Michael Naranjo's sculpture on these two pages shows the same artwork from three different views. Blinded in Vietnam, Naranjo's ideas come from things he saw in his past. The views of *Eagle's Song* from three different angles show his ability to create a three-dimensional piece of art from memory.

Michael Naranjo. Santa Clara Pueblo (American). *Eagle's Song.* Bronze.
Photography by © 1995 Mark Nohl.

Look at the different views of the sculpture.

✓ What part of the sculpture do you notice first in each view?

✓ How do the shapes change in the different views?

✓ How do the shadows and highlights change?

SEEING LIKE AN ARTIST

Slowly turn your hand holding a pencil. Look at it from different angles. How does the pencil change as you turn it? How does your hand change as you turn it?

Using Point of View

Point of view is the angle from which the viewer sees an object. The shapes and forms a viewer sees depend on his or her point of view. There are four common points of view: front view, back view, side view, and overhead view.

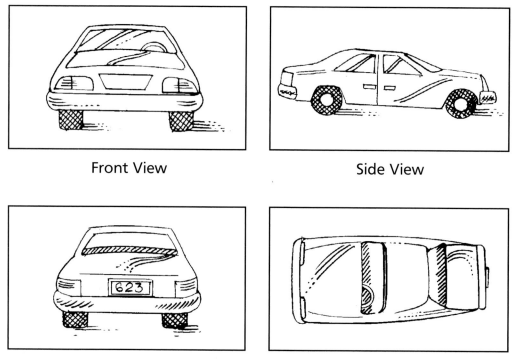

Front View

Side View

Back View

Overhead View

Notice how your perception changes as you look at the same object from different points of view.

Practice

Describe an object from two different points of view. Use pencil.

1. Fold a sheet of paper in half. Label each half with the point of view you will be using. Select an object from your desk and study it carefully from two different points of view.

2. Write down the parts of the object you see from each view.

Decide How many parts of the object could you see from both points of view? Which point of view showed the most interesting shape?

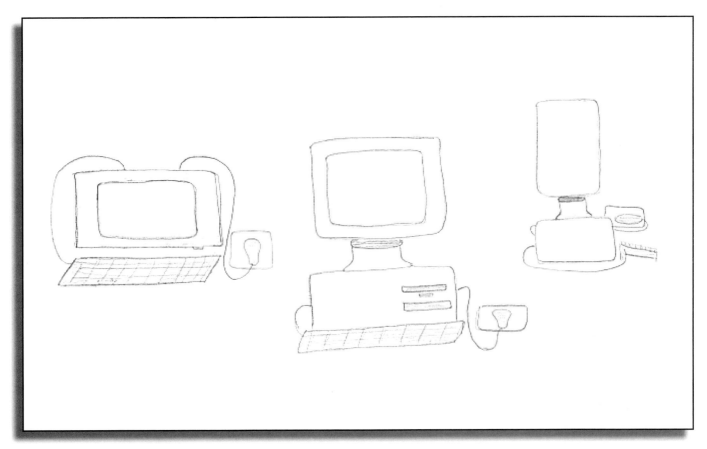

Vicki Lester. Age 9. Pencil.

What object did this student draw? What three points of view were used?

Create

What object would make an interesting subject to photograph from three different views? Photograph a three-dimensional object from three points of view.

1. Think about three-dimensional objects you would like to photograph. Select one.

2. Look carefully at the object you have chosen. Place it in front of you. Walk around it, stand above it, or lie on the ground and look at it. Choose and photograph your three favorite points of view.

Describe Describe the shapes in your three photographs and how they changed with each different point of view.

Analyze How did you capture shadows and highlights in your photographs?

Interpret What point of view is most interesting? Explain.

Decide What could make your photographs more interesting?

Tactile Texture

Sometimes artists use a variety of materials
to create tactile textures in a work of art.

Artist unknown. Osage (United States).
Woman's Wedding Dress. Cloth, broadcloth,
ribbon, German silver, feather plumes, and
beads. Coat, 120.1 cm long. Sash, 253.6 cm
long. Courtesy of the Smithsonian National
Museum of the American Indian, NY. Photo
by David Heald.

Study the artwork on these two pages. Do you see
anything similar about the two? Both items are made by
the Osage tribe, who migrated to north central Oklahoma
during the 1800s. The feathered hat and elaborate coat you
see are part of an Osage woman's wedding outfit.

Artist unknown. Osage. (United States). *Wedding Hat*. Feathers. 40.7 cm high. Courtesy of the Smithsonian National Museum of the American Indian, NY. Photo by David Heald.

Study both items to find the tactile textures.

- ✓ Describe the materials used in both items.
- ✓ Where do you see a fuzzy texture?
- ✓ Where do you see a rough texture?
- ✓ Locate a smooth texture.

SEEING LIKE AN ARTIST

Look around your classroom for objects with smooth, rough, shiny, and matte textures.

Using Tactile Texture

Tactile texture is an element of art that refers to how things feel. Texture is perceived by touch and sight. The four basic categories of tactile textures are rough, smooth, shiny, and matte.

The textures of objects reflect light differently. The way a surface looks depends on how it reflects light.

Rough-textured surfaces reflect the light unevenly.

Smooth-textured surfaces reflect the light evenly.

Shiny-textured surfaces reflect a bright highlight.

Matte-textured surfaces reflect a light that is soft and dull-looking.

Practice

Collect and reproduce actual textures. Use pencil and crayon.

1. Collect a variety of objects that have the four types of textures. Sort and classify them into the four groups.

2. Select one from each category and, using crayons, make rubbings of these textures.

Decide Look at your textures. Were you able to successfully reproduce each of the actual textures you collected?

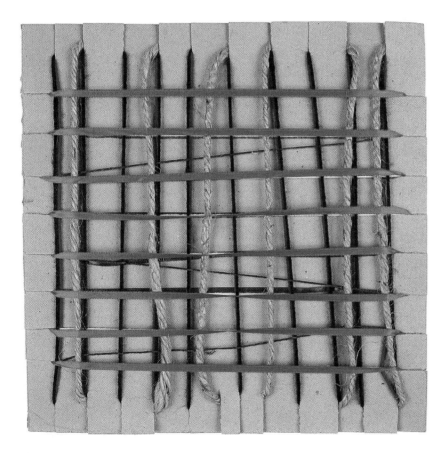

Yolanda Bay. Age 9. Ribbon and yarn.

What textures did this student artist use to create a weaving?

Create

What could you use to make a weaving with texture? Create a weaving using actual textures.

1. Think about materials you could use for a texture weaving. Collect a variety of materials with a variety of textures, such as yarns, ribbons, grasses, leather, and wire.

2. Prepare a piece of cardboard for weaving by notching and stringing the warp threads.

3. Use a variety of textures in your weaving. Think about color variation as you weave.

Describe Describe your weaving.

Analyze What textures did you use to create your weaving? Are their surfaces smooth, rough, shiny, or dull?

Interpret How can you use your weaving?

Decide Did you include a variety of textures in your weaving?

Visual Texture

Artists often create the illusion of texture in a
work of art to show how something feels.

M. C. Escher. (Dutch). *Three Worlds.*
1955. Lithograph. $14\frac{1}{8} \times 9\frac{3}{4}$ inches.
National Gallery of Art,
Washington, DC.

Look at the artworks on these pages. In *Three Worlds,*
Escher used mathematical formulas to carefully
plan his ideas. He was a printmaker who often based his
art on optical illusions and fantasy. Henri Rousseau often
painted scenes of imaginary worlds, too. He filled his
works with exotic plants and animals. Both artists used
visual texture to communicate how the objects might feel
if you could touch them.

Henri Rousseau. (French). *Exotic Landscape.* 1910. Oil on canvas. $51\frac{1}{4} \times 64$ inches. Courtesy of Norton Simon Foundation, Pasadena, California. Photo by Antoni E. Dolinski.

Observe how both artists reproduce textures.

✓ Find repeated lines or shapes. How do these create texture?

✓ Where do you see textures that are furlike?

✓ How was the texture of water created?

✓ What textures does Rousseau create in his painting?

Using Visual Texture

Visual texture is the illusion of a three-dimensional surface based on the memory of how things feel. There are two types of visual texture—invented and simulated.

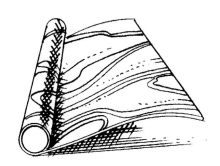

Invented texture is a kind of visual texture that does not represent a real texture but creates the sensation of one by repeating lines and shapes in a two-dimensional pattern.

Simulated texture is a kind of visual texture that imitates real texture by using a two-dimensional pattern to create the illusion of a three-dimensional surface. For example, a plastic tabletop can use a pattern to simulate the texture of wood.

Practice

Identify a simulated and an invented texture. Use magazines.

1. Fold a sheet of white drawing paper in half. Label one side "simulated texture" and the other side "invented texture."

2. Look through magazines and find examples of simulated and invented textures to cut out and glue under your two headings.

Decide Were you able to find magazine examples of both types of visual texture? What differences and similarities do you see?

Becky Crane. Age 9. Crayon and watercolor.

How many rubbings did this student artist make?

Create

How can you use materials found in nature to show texture? Create a painting with a textured surface.

1. Think about the texture of various things found in nature. Collect a variety of natural objects.

2. Test your collected materials by making rubbings on scrap paper. Choose your favorite materials to create your painting.

3. Use warm or cool colors to make rubbings of one material at a time. Fill the paper with an interesting design.

4. Cover your paper with a contrasting watercolor wash.

Describe Describe the shape and textures of your found materials.

Analyze What textures, shapes, and patterns did you use in your painting?

Interpret Give your artwork a title.

Decide How could you add another texture? Were you successfully able to create a painting with a textured surface?

Lesson 6

Texture in the
Oral Tradition

**World Kulintang Institute
Performance Ensemble.**

In ancient times, people passed on their traditions and culture through word of mouth. Storytellers taught the beliefs and values of their people by telling stories. Musicians passed on their songs and rhythms by playing or singing and having young musicians repeat these musical patterns. Their voices and instruments had a variety of textures—smooth, silky, rough, gravelly, and mellow.

Unit **5**

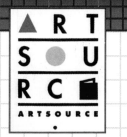
What To Do

Create and learn rhythmic patterns using the oral tradition.

Materials

None

1. Work with a partner. Partner A will create a short rhythmic pattern of sounds using claps, snaps, or stamps. Partner B will repeat the pattern.

2. Create a second pattern of sounds, and follow the same method of teaching and learning.

3. Perform the first and second patterns together in a sequence. You may perform either pattern one or two times before moving on to the next. Do the sequence several times until you can perform it well.

4. Switch roles. Create another sequence of rhythmic patterns.

Describe How did you teach and learn the rhythmic patterns using the oral tradition?

Analyze How did different rhythmic patterns create different textures of sound?

Interpret What feelings did you create with rhythmic patterns?

Decide How well did you succeed in teaching and learning using the oral tradition?

Extra Credit

With your partner, add all four of your patterns together into a longer sequence of rhythm. Perform for the class.

Space and Texture

Reviewing Main Ideas

The lessons and activities in this unit cover the techniques that artists use to create space and texture.

1. **Perspective** is the technique used to create the feeling of depth on a flat piece. There are six perspective techniques.

    - **Overlapping** — When one object covers part of another object, the first object seems closer to the viewer.

    - **Size** — Large objects seem to be closer to the viewer than small objects.

    - **Placement** — Objects placed near the bottom of a picture seem to be closer to the viewer than objects placed higher in the picture.

    - **Detail** — Objects with clear, sharp edges and many details seem to be closer to the viewer. Objects that lack detail and have fuzzy outlines seem to be farther away.

    - **Lines** — Parallel lines seem to move toward the same point as they move farther away from the viewer.

    - **Color** — Brightly colored objects seem closer to the viewer. Objects with pale, dull colors seem to be farther away.

Leon Trousset. (American). *Old Mesilla Plaza.* c. 1865-86. Oil on canvas. $29\frac{9}{16} \times 48\frac{1}{2}$ inches. National Museum of American Art, Washington DC/Art Resource, NY.

2. **Picture plane** is the surface of a drawing. There are three parts of a picture plane—foreground, background, middle ground.

3. **Point of View** is the angle from which the viewer sees an object in artwork.

4. **Tactile Texture** is what artists use to show how things actually feel. (rough, smooth, shiny, matte)

Summing Up

Look at *Old Mesilla Plaza* painted by Leon Trousset. The artist used the techniques covered in this unit to create space and texture.

- Has Trousset used all six perspective techniques? Try to identify at least one example of each technique.
- How many different kinds of textures can you find?
- Does the artist use visual texture to imitate the texture of the wagon, ground, and trees, or does he show the texture of the paint?

Space and texture are important elements in paintings and drawings. By using techniques to create space and textures, artists express to others what they see.

Let's Visit a Museum

The Smithsonian Institution was established in 1846 with funds from the will of the English scientist, James Smithson. Today there are more than 140 million artifacts, exhibits, and works of art at the Smithsonian. It is also a center for research in the arts, sciences, and history. It is made of 16 museums and galleries, several research centers, and the National Zoo. Nine of the museums are located on the National Mall in Washington, DC, between the Capitol and Washington Monument.

The Smithsonian Institution

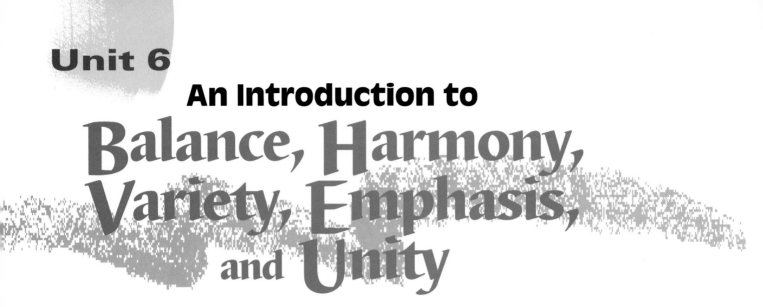

Unit 6

An Introduction to
Balance, Harmony, Variety, Emphasis, and Unity

Artists use balance, harmony, variety, and unity to create interest in a work of art.

Chartres Cathedral.
Chartres, France. 1134–1220.

Artists use **balance, harmony,** and **variety** in architecture to create **unity.**

- Look at the front of the cathedral. What objects are the same on both sides?
- Which parts of the cathedral are not exactly the same?
- When you look at Chartres Cathedral, what is the first thing you see? Why do you think you see this item first?
- Which shapes do you see more than once?
- What creates the feeling of wholeness in the cathedral?

Artist **P**rofile
Chartres Cathedral

The Rose Window.

The Chartres Cathedral is located in France, in a small town southwest of Paris called Chartres. This is the sixth church to be built on the site. The last church was destroyed in a fire, leaving only the front of the building and the south tower. The rebuilding of the present cathedral began in 1194 and ended in 1220, a total of 27 years. Chartres Cathedral is one of the most famous churches in the world. It is particularly noted for the beauty of its stained glass windows.

Architects and artists use balance, harmony, and variety to help them create unity in a work of art. In this unit you will learn and practice the techniques that artists use to create unity in their artwork. Here are the topics you will study:

- Balance
- Harmony
- Emphasis
- Variety
- Unity

Formal Balance

Formal balance is used by artists to create stability in a work of art.

Artist unknown. Maori (New Zealand). *Figure from House Post.* 19th century. Wood. 43 inches. Metropolitan Museum of Art, New York, New York. C. Rockefeller Memorial Collection, Bequest of Nelson A. Rockefeller, 1979.

Both images on these pages show examples of formal balance. *Figure from House Post* was carved by a Maori artist of New Zealand. The *Tree-house Folly* was made more than 200 years ago. A folly, in England, is a building built for fun. Notice how it is placed in the largest "V" shape in the tree.

Artist unknown. (England).*Tree-house Folly.* Permission courtesy Random House, Inc. Alfred A. Knopf, Inc. Photographer Ken Kirkwood.

Study both artworks to find examples of formal balance.

- Where do you see repeated lines, shapes, forms, or colors?

- What similarities do you see within each individual work of art?

- If you could draw a line down the center of each, dividing it in half, would there be any similarities between the two halves?

SEEING LIKE AN ARTIST

Think about objects you see every day that, when divided in half, would look the same on both sides.

Using Formal Balance

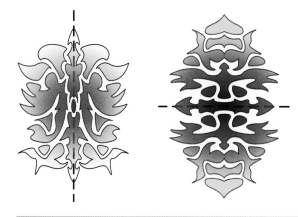

Formal balance is a way of organizing parts of a design so that equal, or very similar, elements are placed on opposite sides of a central line. This central line may be part of the design or an imaginary line.

Symmetry is a type of formal balance in which two halves of an object or composition are mirror images of each other.

Practice

Create a design using formal balance. Use colored pencils.

1. Begin with a central line drawn down the middle of your paper.

2. Draw each side so that your design is a mirror image of the other.

Decide Does your design illustrate formal balance?

Fred Ramey. Age 9. Crayon.

How could this student artist use formal balance to add more details to the artwork?

Create

If you could build a tree house, what would you like it to look like? Use formal balance to design a tree house.

1. Think about a tree house design.

2. First, draw your tree. Use formal balance to divide the trunk with a large "V" shape in the center. You may choose to use *Treetop Folly* as an example.

3. Then, design your tree house using formal balance. Trace over all your lines with black crayon.

Describe What types of shapes and lines did you use?

Analyze How did you create formal balance?

Interpret What name best describes your tree house?

Decide Do you like the way your design turned out? Do you feel you were successful in creating formal balance in your design? Why?

Informal Balance

Sometimes artists use informal balance
to create a work of art.

Jessica Hines. (American).
Spirit of Place Series #26.

Look at the photograph and painting on these pages.
Spirit of Place Series #26 shows a desert landscape
photographed in the Southwest. The Jakuchū painting
uses exaggeration to illustrate intelligence and wisdom.
Both works of art illustrate informal balance.

Itō Jakuchū. (Japanese). *Fúkurōjin, The God of Longevity and Wisdom.* 1790. Ink on scroll. $45\frac{5}{8} \times 22\frac{1}{4}$ inches. Los Angeles County Museum of Art, Los Angeles, California.

Study informal balance in both artworks.

☑ If you could draw a line down the center of each of these artworks and divide them in half, what differences would you see in the two halves?

☑ Which side of Jessica Hines's artwork has more objects than the other?

☑ What appears to be closest to the front in each artwork?

☑ What is the empty space in each artwork?

SEEING LIKE AN ARTIST

Look at your teacher's desk. Do you see formal or informal balance?

Using Informal Balance

Informal balance, or **asymmetry**, can be seen, not measured. Artists use informal balance to organize parts of a design so that objects have equal visual weight.

Visual weight cannot be measured on a scale. It is measured by which object your eye sees first. Differences in color, shape, and contour affect visual weight.

Bright colors have more visual weight than dull colors.

Large shapes have more visual weight than small shapes.

A busy **contour**, or border, has more visual weight than a smooth contour.

Position, or placement, can be used to create informal balance.

Practice

Use a balance scale to create informal balance.

1. Gather various objects from around the classroom.

2. Create informal balance by adding different combinations of objects onto the scale.

Decide What objects did you add onto each side of the scale to create informal balance?

Melissa Hintzman. Age 9. Oil pastels and watercolors.

Think of a name for this student artist's planet.

Create

What vegetation might you find on an imaginary inhabited planet? Create a planetscape using informal balance.

1. Think about the vegetation and land mass you want on your planet.

2. Make several sketches of objects you might like to include in your planetscape. Choose one.

3. Use informal balance to organize the objects. Place one large object near the center on one half of the paper, and place several small objects far from the center on the other half.

4. Add color to your planetscape.

Describe Describe the land and vegetation in your planetscape.

Analyze Discuss how you organized the objects to create informal balance.

Interpret What mood was created in your landscape?

Decide Would this planetscape have the same mood if it had formal balance?

Radial Balance

Artists often use radial designs in their artwork.

Artist unknown. (Chinese). *Carved Lacquer Circular Tray*. Song Dynasty. 1127–1279. Black, red, and yellow lacquer on wood. $2\frac{1}{16} \times 13\frac{3}{4}$ inches. Courtesy of the Arthur M. Sackler Gallery, Smithsonian Institution, Washington, DC.

The tray and the plate on these pages are examples of radial balance. *Carved Lacquer Circular Tray* was made by carving a design through lacquer painted on wood. The design on *Pottery Plate, Black on Black Feather Design* is called *puname,* or the "eagle feather" pattern. Notice how the design on both works of art radiates out from the center in a circular design.

Maria Martínez and Popovi Da. Tewa (American). *Pottery Plate, Black on Black Feather Design.* Pottery. Courtesy Dennis and Janis Lyon, Maria Martínez, © Jerry Jacka Photograpy.

Look closely at the two works of art to find radial design.

✓ Where do the designs begin?

✓ If you turn the book, do the designs change? Do they stay the same?

✓ What is the difference in the types of lines each artist used?

SEEING LIKE AN ARTIST

What are some objects in nature that are circular in shape, such as a flower? What are some objects that are made by people, such as an open umbrella?

Using Radial Balance

Radial balance occurs when the elements in a design (line, shape, color, or form) **radiate**, or come out, from one central point. It is an example of **symmetry** because both sides of the design are mirror images of each other.

You can find radial balance both in nature and in objects made by people. If you look closely at a flower, you will see that the petals are often arranged around a central point. The face of a clock also shows radial balance.

Practice

Find examples of radial designs in your classroom. Use paper.

1. Divide a sheet of paper into two columns.

2. Label the first column "Nature" and the second column "Human-made."

3. List examples of radial balance in the correct column.

Decide Were you able to find examples of radial designs found both in nature and made by people? How are they alike?

Carrie Eldridge. Age 9. Fine-tip markers.

What other objects in nature could this student artist have used to create a radial design?

Create

What objects in nature have interesting shapes? Create a radial design using several shapes.

1. Think of radial designs found in nature and make a list of these objects.

2. Make several sketches of the objects from your list. Choose one to reproduce as a simple radial design.

3. Draw an 8-inch circle and divide it into four sections. Start drawing your radial design in one section. After you are finished, continue drawing your design in the other three sections. The objects should all come from the center of the circle.

4. Complete the design in color.

Describe Describe your design and the lines, shapes, and colors used to create it.

Analyze Describe how you used the elements of nature to think of ideas for your radial design.

Interpret What could your design be used for?

Decide Were you able to create a radial design? Why or why not? What changes would you make to improve your design?

Harmony

Harmony is an element used to create sculpture.

Artist unknown. (India). *Shiva as Lord of the Dance/India Tamil, Nadu Chola/#1979–20.*
c. 970. 12th century. Copper alloy. 29$\frac{1}{4}$ inches height. The Asia Society, New York,
Mr. and Mrs. John D. Rockefeller 3rd Collection/Photo by Lynton Gardiner.

The artworks on these pages are forms of sculpture. *Shiva as Lord of the Dance* was made from copper and carried in a religious parade. *Cantileve* was made from natural forms that were cast in metal. Both sculptures show examples of harmony.

Nancy Graves. (American) *Cantileve.* 1983. Bronze with polychrome patina. 98 × 68 × 54 inches. Collection of Whitney Museum of American Art, Purchase with funds from the Painting and Sculpture Committee. New York, New York.

Look closely at both sculptures.

- ✓ What appears to circle *Shiva?*
- ✓ What shapes or forms are repeated in each sculpture?
- ✓ How did Graves use color?
- ✓ What things from nature can you see in *Cantileve?*

SEEING LIKE AN ARTIST

Look through this book for other sculptures. Compare the two sculptures in this lesson to others you find.

Using Harmony

Harmony is the principle of design that creates unity by stressing similarities of separate but related parts.

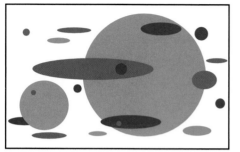

Repetition of shapes can be used in a work of art to create harmony.

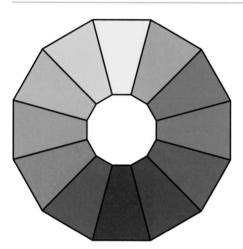

Analogous colors create harmony. They are colors that sit next to each other on the color wheel and have a common color such as violet, red-violet, and red or green, blue-green, blue, and blue-violet.

An **assemblage** is a three-dimensional work of art made of many pieces put together. An artist can make an assemblage harmonious by using related shapes or colors.

Practice

Build a temporary sculpture on your desk that shows harmony. Use objects from your desk.

1. Create a harmonious sculpture using several objects.

2. Take your sculpture apart and build it another way.

Decide Did you successfully create a design that shows harmony?

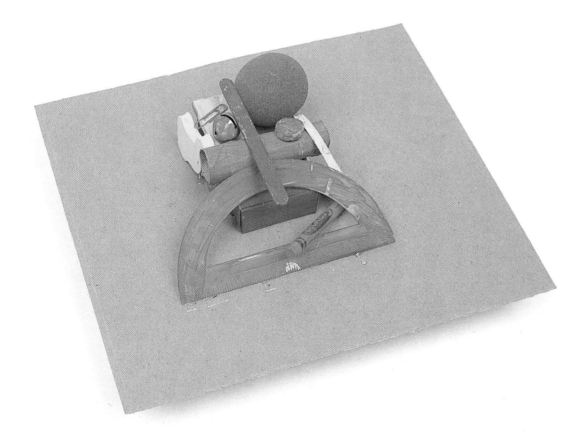

Cecilia Bonilla. Age 9. Mixed media.

How has this student artist created harmony?

Create

What type of sculpture would fit your school setting? Create a model of a sculpture using harmony.

1. Think of the type of sculpture that would fit the environment of your school. Choose an appropriate site for your sculpture.

2. Draw several sketches of how you want your sculpture to look. Select one sketch as your plan.

3. Using cardboard and found objects, build a model of your sculpture. Use analogous colors to create harmony in your design.

Describe Describe the materials you used to create your model and the site you chose.

Analyze How did you create harmony in your sculpture?

Interpret Give your sculpture a title.

Decide Does your model have harmony?

Lesson 4

Variety and Emphasis

Artists often use variety and emphasis to create a work of art.

Nancy Holt. (American). *Sun Tunnels*. 1973–76. Four huge concrete pipes. 86 feet overall. Great Basin Desert, Utah. Courtesy of the John Weber Gallery, NY.

Look at the structures on these pages. Both are examples of **environmental art**, art that is created to be part of a landscape. *Sun Tunnels* blends with its desert environment and glows with sunlight. The $24\frac{1}{2}$-mile *Running Fence* wraps the contour of a California landscape. It was in place for only 12 days.

Javacheff Christo and Jeanne-Claude. (Bulgarian). *Running Fence.* 1972–76. Nylon fabric and steel cables and poles. 18 feet high, 24$\frac{1}{2}$ miles long. Installed for 12 days. Sonoma and Marin Counties, California. © Christo 1976 Photo: Wolfgang Volz.

tudy both artworks to see how the artists create variety.

✓ How does each artwork make you notice the environment?

✓ What do you observe about each artist's use of color?

✓ Do these artworks fit or blend with their environments?

SEEING LIKE AN ARTIST

What would your house look like if it were wrapped with fabric?

Using Variety and Emphasis

Variety is created in art through differences and contrasts.

Simplicity means limiting the number of elements in an artwork.

Emphasis is a principle of design that makes one part of the artwork stand out more than the other parts. The element that is noticed first is the **dominant element**.

Practice

Use your initials to show simplicity and variety. Use crayon.

1. Fold a sheet of white drawing paper into two sections. In the first section, draw one design of your initials that shows simplicity. You might use simple lines and just one color.

2. In the second box, draw an initial design that shows variety. You might draw different patterns or use contrasts in color.

Decide Do your designs show simplicity and variety? Which design do you like best? Why?

What objects do you think this student artist wrapped?

Adrianne Hopp. Age 9.
Red Cover on a Chair. Fabric.

Create

What could you use to create a wrapped sculpture? Create a wrapped sculpture to show emphasis.

1. Think about unusual materials you could use to wrap an object.

2. With a small group of classmates, choose one or two objects to wrap. Discuss the different materials you could use to wrap your objects.

Describe Describe the objects and materials you used to create a wrapped sculpture.

Analyze How did wrapping the object emphasize its form? Did the wrapping change your view of the objects?

Interpret How did wrapping change the use of the object?

Decide What else would you like to use to wrap your objects?

Unity

Artists balance harmony and variety to create unity.

Brower Hatcher. (American). *Prophecy of the Ancients.* 1988. Cast stone, stainless steel, steel, bronze, and aluminum. 202 × 246 inches. Collection Walker Art Center, Minneapolis, Minnesota. Gift of the Lilly Family, 1989.

Look at the architectural sculptures on these pages. Brower Hatcher's *Prophecy of the Ancients* ties together ancient columns and a modern dome to create unity. *Spoon Bridge and Cherry* blends everyday objects with the environment. Both artists used harmony and variety to create unity in their work.

Claes Oldenburg (Swedish) and **Coosje van Bruggen**. (Dutch). *Spoon Bridge and Cherry*. 1985.
Stainless steel, aluminum, and paint. Collection Walker Art Center, Minneapolis, Minnesota.
Gift of Frederick R. Weisman in honor of his parents, William and Mary Weisman, 1988.

Study the sculptures on these two pages to find examples of unity.

☑ What shapes do you see in each of these sculptures?

☑ How does each sculpture fit its environment?

☑ How does Hatcher make the viewer connect the ground to the sky?

☑ How does *Spoon Bridge and Cherry* connect with the environment?

SEEING LIKE AN ARTIST
Have you ever seen a sculpture that is similar to either sculpture in this lesson?

Using Unity

Harmony is the principle of design that creates unity by stressing similarities of separate but related parts.

Variety is the principle of design that is concerned with difference or contrast.

Unity is oneness. It brings order to the world. It helps you focus on a work of art as a whole instead of its individual parts. Unity helps you see what different parts of a design have in common and how they belong together.

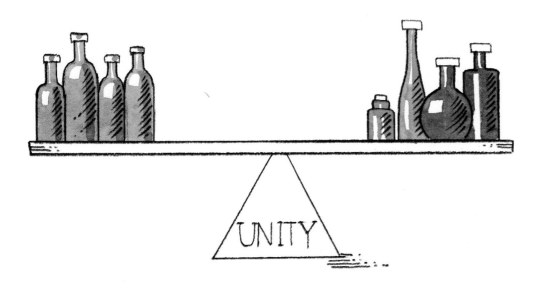

Practice

Look at advertisements in magazines for examples of harmony, variety, and unity. Use magazines and scissors.

1. Look through magazines for examples of harmony, variety, and unity.

2. On a sheet of paper, arrange examples of each. Place them under the headings "Harmony," "Variety," and "Unity."

Decide Were you able to identify harmony, variety, and unity?

Brett Altizer. Age 9. Found natural objects.

What would make a good title for this diorama?

Create

How can you make a common everyday object into a sculpture? Create a diorama using a piece of sculpture that connects with its environment.

1. Think about an everyday object that would make an interesting sculpture.

2. Draw some sketches of your object in an outdoor environment, making sure to include elements of harmony, variety, and unity in your designs.

3. Choose one sketch to use in building an environmental diorama where you can place your object. Use a variety of materials.

Describe Describe the objects you chose for your sculpture.

Analyze What object did you use to unify your object in the diorama?

Interpret Is your sculpture funny or serious?

Decide How would your sculpture fit in a real environment?

Balance, Harmony, Variety, and Unity in Dance

Lily Cai Chinese Dance Company: *"The Flying Goddess."*

ily Cai performs traditional dances from ancient Chinese culture. In the picture above, she performs a Chinese ribbon dance called "The Flying Goddess." The flying and floating of the red ribbons represent the spirit of a goddess. The dance patterns are based on circles. The dancer moves in a variety of visual patterns. She creates balance, harmony, variety, and unity in her dance.

What To Do

Create your own ribbon dance.

Materials
✓ thin wooden dowels or plastic straws
✓ crepe paper or ribbons
✓ tape or staples

1. Attach the crepe paper or ribbons to the dowel.

2. Try twirling the ribbon by making large circle patterns on different sides of your body and in different directions.

3. Next, make large figure-eight patterns in different directions and positions. Then, combine the circles and figure eights in different ways.

4. Work out your own ribbon dance by selecting four to six different patterns. Work to achieve balance, harmony, variety, and unity.

Describe Describe the visual patterns you created as you moved with your ribbon.

Analyze How did you create balance, harmony, variety, and unity in your movements?

Interpret What feelings did you create in your ribbon dance?

Decide How well do you think you succeeded in creating your ribbon dance?

Extra Credit

Try adding jumps, turns, and traveling movements as you work with the ribbons. Then, select music and perform your dance for others.

Balance, Harmony, Variety, Emphasis, and Unity

Reviewing Main Ideas

The lessons and activities in this unit are based on a number of ways artists use balance, harmony, and variety to create unity in works of art.

1. **Formal balance** occurs when equal, or very similar, elements are placed on opposite sides of a central line. When the two halves are mirror images of each other, it is called **symmetry.**

2. **Informal balance,** or **asymmetry,** is a way of organizing parts of a design so that they have equal visual weight.

   • Bright colors have more visual weight than dull colors.

   • Large shapes have more visual weight than small shapes.

   • A busy contour has more visual weight than a smooth contour.

3. **Radial balance** is an example of symmetry. It occurs when the elements of design (line, shape, color, form) radiate, or come out, from a central point.

Elsa Schaparelli. (Italian). *Coat.* 1939. Silk. Metropolitan Museum of Art, New York, New York. Gift of Mrs. Pauline Potter, 1950. Photograph by Mark Darley.

4. **Harmony** is the principle of design that creates unity by stressing similarities of separate but related parts. *Analogous colors* create harmony.

5. **Variety** is created in art through differences or contrasts.

6. **Emphasis** is the principle of design that makes one part of the artwork stand out more than the others.

7. **Unity** is the wholeness or oneness created in a work of art.

Summing Up

Coat by Elsa Schaparelli was designed using formal balance which is covered in this unit.

• Describe the type of balance used in this work of art. How are the art elements of line, shape, and color arranged?

• What area is emphasized or seems to stand out? How do you think the artist created this emphasis?

• What elements unify, or bring all the parts together?

• What feeling do you get when you look at this work of art? Do you like it? Why or why not?

Balance, harmony, variety, and unity are important elements in art. By using techniques to create balance, harmony, variety, and unity, artists make a work of art more interesting by bringing all the parts together.

Careers in Art
Fashion Designer

Carolina Herrera is a fashion designer who lives and works in New York City. When she was a little girl, she was fascinated by the clothes the characters were wearing in the books she read. What she likes best about her work is creating a new collection of clothes, which involves developing the designs and choosing the fabrics and colors. She prepared for her career by taking courses in fashion design, which included fabrics, sketching, draping, and pattern making.

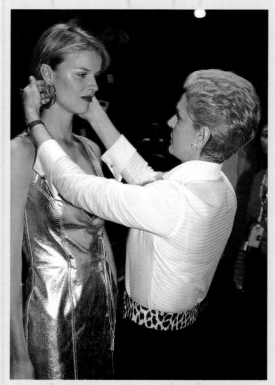

Carolina Herrera, fashion designer

Technique Tips

Pencil

With the side of your pencil lead, press harder and shade over areas more than once for darker values. With a pencil, you can add form to your objects by shading. You can also use lines or dots for shading. When lines or dots are drawn close together, you get darker values. When dots or lines are drawn farther apart, lighter values are created.

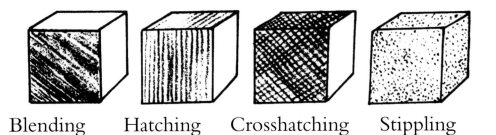

Blending   Hatching   Crosshatching   Stippling

Colored Pencil

You can blend colors with colored pencils. Color with the lighter color first. Gently color over it with the darker color until you have the effect you want.

With colored pencils, you can use the four shading techniques shown above.

Shadows or darker values can be created by blending complementary colors.

Technique Tips

Felt-tip Pen

Felt-tip pens can be used to make either sketches or finished drawings. They are ideal for contour drawings.

Use the point of a felt-tip pen to make details.

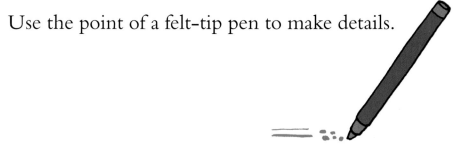

Felt-tip pens can be used for hatching, cross-hatching, and stippling.

Hatching   Cross-hatching   Stippling

Always replace the cap so the felt-tip pen doesn't dry out.

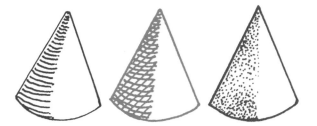

Technique Tips

Marker

Markers can be used to make sketches or finished drawings. Use the point of the marker to make thin lines and small dots.

Use the side of the tip for coloring in areas and for making thick lines.

Always replace the cap so the marker doesn't dry out.

Technique Tips

Colored Chalk

Colored chalks can be used to make colorful, soft designs.

You can use the tip of the colored chalk to create lines, color shapes, and fill spaces. As with pencil, you can also use them for blending to create shadows.

Colored chalk is soft and can break easily. These pieces are still usable. Colors can be mixed or blended by smearing them together with your finger or a tissue.

Oil Pastels

Oil pastels are colors that are mixed with oil and pressed into sticks. When you press down hard with them, your pictures will look painted.

Oil pastels are soft. You can use oil pastels to color over other media, such as tempera or crayon. Then, you can scratch through this covering to create a design.

More About...
Technique Tips

Tempera

1. Fill water containers halfway. Dip your brush in water. Wipe your brush on the inside edge of the container. Then, blot it on a paper towel to get rid of extra water. Stir the paints. Add a little water if a color is too thick or dry. Remember to clean your brush before using a new color.

2. Always mix colors on a palette. Put some of each color that you want to mix on the palette. Then, add the darker color a little at a time to the lighter color. Change your water when it gets too muddy.

3. To create lighter values, add white. To darken a value, add a tiny amount of black. If you have painted something too thickly, add water and blot it with a clean paper towel.

4. Use a thin, pointed brush to paint thin lines and details. For thick lines or large areas, press firmly on the tip or use a wide brush.

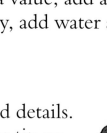

5. Wash your brushes when you are done. Reshape the bristles. Store brushes with the bristles up.

More About...
Technique Tips

Watercolor

1. Fill water containers halfway. Dip your brush in water. Wipe your brush on the inside edge of the container. Then blot it on a paper towel to get rid of extra water. With your brush, add a drop of water to each watercolor cake and stir. Remember to clean your brush whenever you change colors.

2. Always mix colors on a palette. Put some of each color that you want to mix on the palette. Then, add the darker color a little at a time to the lighter color. Change your water when it gets too muddy.

3. To create lighter values, add more water. To darken a value, add a tiny amount of black. If you have painted something too thickly, add water and blot it with a clean paper towel.

4. Use a thin, pointed brush to paint thin lines and details. For thick lines or large areas, press firmly on the tip or use a wide brush.

5. For a softer look, tape your paper to the table with masking tape. Use a wide brush to add water to the paper, working in rows from top to bottom. This is a **wash.** Let the water soak in a little. Painting on wet paper will create a soft or fuzzy look. For sharper forms or edges, paint on dry paper, using only a little water on your brush.

6. Wash your brushes when you are done. Reshape the bristles. Store brushes with the bristles up.

Technique Tips

Printmaking: Making Stamps

Two methods for making stamps for printmaking are listed below. You can cut either a positive or negative shape into most of these objects. Be sure to talk with your teacher or another adult about what kind of tools you can use safely.

- Cut sponges into shapes.

- Draw or sculpt a design on a flat piece of modeling clay using a pencil, clay tool, tip of a paper clip, or other object.

More About...

Technique Tips

Printmaking: Printing Stamps

1. Put a small amount of water-based printing ink or some paint onto a hard, flat surface. Roll a soft roller, called a brayer, back and forth in the ink until there is an even coating of paint on both the surface and the brayer.

2. Brush the ink on with a flat, wide brush also. The ink should cover the stamp evenly without going into the grooves of your design.

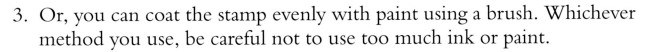

3. Or, you can coat the stamp evenly with paint using a brush. Whichever method you use, be careful not to use too much ink or paint.

4. Gently press your stamp carefully onto your paper. Then, peel the paper and stamp apart and check your print. If you wish to make several prints of your design, you should ink your stamp again as needed.

5. When you have finished, wash the brayer, surface, and stamp.

Technique Tips

Collage

In a collage, objects or pieces of paper, fabric, or other materials are pasted onto a surface to create a work of art. When planning your collage, consider such things as:

- Size of shapes and spaces

- Placement of shapes and spaces

- Color schemes

- Textures

Remember that the empty (negative) spaces are also part of your design. Plan a collage as you would plan a painting or drawing. After deciding what shapes and objects you want to use, arrange them on the paper. When you have made an arrangement you like, glue your shapes and objects to the paper.

Technique Tips

Papier-Mâché—Strip Method

The strip method of papier-mâché ("mashed paper") uses paper combined with paste. Often, papier-mâché is molded over a form that helps it keep its shape while it's drying.

1. Create a supporting form, if needed. Forms can be made from clay, wadded-up newspaper, cardboard boxes and tubes, balloons, wire, or other materials. Masking tape can be used to hold the form together.

2. Tear paper into strips. Either dip the strips into a thick mixture of paste or rub paste on the strips with your fingers. Use wide strips to cover wide forms and thin strips or small pieces to cover a small shape.

3. To remove the form when the papier-mâché is dry, first cover it with plastic wrap or a layer of wet newspaper strips.

Then, apply five or six layers of strips. Lay each layer in a different direction so you can keep track of the number of strips and layers. For example, lay the first layer vertically and the second horizontally. Smooth over all rough edges with your fingers. If you are going to leave the form in place permanently, two or three layers of strips should be enough.

4. When it is dry, you can paint your sculpture.

Technique Tips

Clay

1. Pinch and pull clay into the desired shape.

2. To join two pieces of clay together:

   • *Score,* or scratch, both pieces so they will stick together.

   • Attach the pieces with some *slip,* which is watery clay.

   • *Squeeze* the two pieces together.

   • *Smooth* the edges.

3. To carve a design out of clay, scratch or dig out your design with a paper clip or other tools.

4. To roll a slab of clay, press a ball of clay into a flat shape on a cloth-covered board. Place one 1/4" slat on each side of the clay. Use a roller to press the slab into an even thickness. With a straightened paper clip, trim the slab into the desired shape.

5. Wrap unfinished sculptures in plastic to keep them moist until you are finished.

Technique Tips

Soap and Plaster Sculpture

You can carve sculptures from clay, soap, or plaster forms. Draw the basic shape of your idea onto all sides of the form. Keep your design simple. Carve a little bit at a time, using a spoon, a paper clip, or plastic knife, while turning your form constantly.

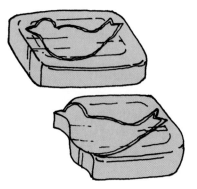

More About...
Art Criticism

Carmen Lomas Garza. (American). *Cakewalk*. 1987. Acrylics. 36 × 48 inches.
Collection of Paula Maciel-Beneke and Norbert Beneke, Soquel, CA. Photo by M. Lee Fatherree.

DESCRIBE

Make a list of all the things you see in this painting.

ANALYZE

Discuss the way the artist has used line, shape, color, value, space, and texture.

How has the artist used rhythm, balance, emphasis, variety, and harmony to organize this work of art?

Carmen Lomas Garza. (American). *Cakewalk.* 1987. Acrylics. 36 × 48 inches.
Collection of Paula Maciel-Beneke and Norbert Beneke, Soquel, CA. Photo by M. Lee Fatherree.

INTERPRET

**What is happening? What is the
artist telling you about the people
and the neighborhood that they
live in?**

DECIDE

**Have you ever seen another work of
art that looks like this painting?**

**Is this painting successful because
it is realistic?**

**Is it successful because it is
well-organized?**

**Is it successful because you have
strong feelings when you study it?**

LOOK

Carmen Lomas Garza. (American). *Cakewalk*. 1987. Acrylics. 36 × 48 inches.
Collection of Paula Maciel-Beneke and Norbert Beneke, Soquel, CA. Photo by M. Lee Fatherree.

LOOK AGAIN

Look at the work of art.

What sounds are in this work of art?

What music are they playing?

What smells are in this work of art?

If you could take away from or add images or elements to the work of art, what would they be and why?

What happened just before and just after in this work of art?

LOOK INSIDE

Look at the work of art.

Think of three ideas or symbols that tell about it.

If you could join these people, who would you like to be?

What would you do in this scene?

Describe what you can't see that is on the street to the right and left.

Act out or show the story in the work of art with a beginning, a middle, and an end.

Carmen Lomas Garza. (American). *Cakewalk.* 1987. Acrylics. 36 × 48 inches. Collection of Paula Maciel-Beneke and Norbert Beneke, Soquel, CA. Photo by M. Lee Fatherree.

LOOK OUTSIDE

Look at the work of art.

How is this like or different from your own life?

How would you change this work of art to be more like your life? What would the changes be? What would the artwork look like?

What does the artist want you to know or think about in this work of art?

Describe your journey about viewing this work of art. Include your thoughts, ideas, and changes in thinking.

Describe the neighborhood and town in this work of art. What are the people like?

What will you remember about this work?

Artist unknown.
Adena Effigy Figure.
100–300 B.C. United States.

Artist unknown.
Three Cows and One Horse.
15,000–13,000 B.C. France.

Artist unknown.
Statues from Abu Temple.
2700–2000 B.C. Iraq.

Artist unknown.
Tutankhamen Mask (side view).
c. 1340 B.C. Egypt.

Artist unknown.
Kuang.
1100 B.C. China.

Artist unknown.
Colossal Head.
1500–300 B.C. Mexico.

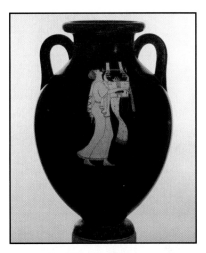

Artist unknown.
Woman Playing Harp.
(Detail from vase.) c. 490 B.C.

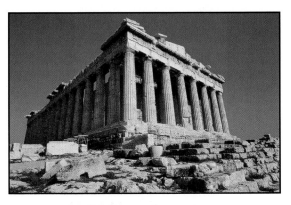

Artist unknown.
Parthenon.
448–432 B.C. Greece.

Artist unknown.
Stonehenge.
1800–1400 B.C. England.

More About...Art History

Artist unknown.
Shiva as Lord of the Dance.
1000. India.

Artist unknown.
Ravenna Apse Mosaic. (Detail).
A.D. 100. Italy.

Artist unknown.
The Pantheon.
A.D. 118–125. Italy.

Artist unknown.
Hagia Sophia.
A.D. 532–537. Turkey.

Artist unknown.
The Great Stupa (at Sanchi).
200–100 B.C. India.

Artist unknown.
Page from *The Book of Lindisfarne*.
Late 600s. England.

Artist unknown.
*Pagoda of the Temple
of the Six Banyan Trees.*
A.D. 537. China.

Artist unknown.
Stupa (at Borobudu).
800. Indonesia.

Artist unknown.
Great Mosque
(at Samarra).
648–852. Iraq.

Rembrandt van Rijn.
Self-Portrait.
1660. The Netherlands.

Leonardo da Vinci.
Mona Lisa.
1503–1505. Italy.

Artist unknown.
Bayon Temple Angkor Thom.
1100s–1200s. Cambodia.

Artist unknown.
Shrine Head. (Yorub).
1100–1300. Nigeria.

Torii Kiyotada.
Actor of the Ichikawa Clan.
1710–1740. Japan.

Artist unknown.
Chartes Cathedral.
1145–1220. France.

Thomas Jefferson.
Monticello.
1770–1784. United States.

Artist unknown.
Bayeux Tapestry. (Detail).
1070–1080. England.

Artist unknown.
Anasazi culture petroglyphs.
United States.

Artist unknown.
Taj Mahal.
1632–1648. India.

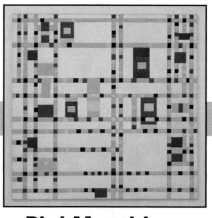

Piet Mondrian.
Broadway Boogie-Woogie.
1941. The Netherlands.

Claude Monet.
Impression, Sunrise.
1872. France.

Edgar Degas.
Little Dancer of Fourteen.
1880–1881. France.

Katsushika Hokusai.
The Great Wave.
1823–1829. Japan.

Pablo Picasso.
Gertrude Stein.
1906. Spain.

Chuck Close.
Self-Portrait.
1987. United States.

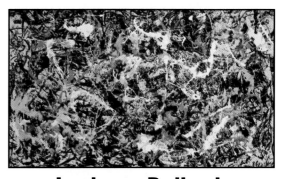

Jackson Pollock.
Convergence.
1952. United States.

Maria Martinez.
Black on Black Pot.
1920. United States.

Alexander Calder.
Untitled Mobile.
1959. United States.

More About...Art History

More About...
Subject Matter

Subject matter is the content of an artist's artwork. Some subject matter is easy to identify. For example, the subject of a painting can be a still life or a portrait. Identifying the subject matter becomes more difficult when the artwork stands for something beyond itself. Look at the artwork on these pages. Notice the different words used to identify different kinds of subject matter.

Still Life

David Hockney. (British). *Mount Fuji and Flowers.* 1972. Acrylic on canvas. 60 × 48 inches. Metropolitan Museum of Art, New York. Purchase, Mrs. Arthur Hays Sulzberger Gift, 1972. Photograph by Lynton Gardiner. © David Hockney.

More About...
Subject Matter

Portrait

Gilbert Stuart. (American). *George Washington*. 1797.
Pennsylvania Academy of Fine Arts.

More About...
Subject **M**atter

Symbolic

Childe Hassam. (American).
Avenue of the Allies, Great Britain.
1918. Oil on canvas.
$36 \times 28\frac{3}{4}$ inches. Metropolitan
Museum of Art, New York. Bequest
of Miss Adelaide Milton de Groot
(1876–1967) 1967.

Allegory

Jan van Eyck. (Flemish).
Giovanni Arnolfini and His Bride.
1434. Tempera and oil on wood.
$33 \times 23\frac{1}{2}$ inches. Courtesy of the
Trustee of the National Gallery,
London, England.

Subject Matter

Nonobjective

Max Weber. (American). *Chinese Restaurant.* 1915.
Oil on canvas. 40 × 48 inches. The Whitney Museum of
Modern Art, New York, New York.

Landscape

Grant Wood. (American). *The Midnight Ride of Paul Revere.*
1931. Oil on composition board. 30 × 40 inches.
Metropolitan Museum of Art, New York, Arthur Hoppock
Heam Fund, 1960. © 1998 Estate of Grant Wood/
Licensed by VAGA, New York, NY.

More About...
Subject Matter

Genre

James Tissot. (French). *A Passing Storm.* c. 1875.
Beaverbrook Art Gallery, Frederickton, New Brunswick, Canada.

More About...
Still-Life Drawing

Everything you see is filled with lines and shapes you already know how to draw.

More About...
Still-Life Drawing

LOOK

Look at the photograph of the still life.

- ☑ Find the horizontal lines on the edge of the table.
- ☑ Find the vertical lines on the sides of the red box.
- ☑ Find the diagonal lines on the top and bottom edges of the red box. Because you see three sides of the box at once, you can tell that it is a form.
- ☑ Find the curved line in the jump rope. Find these lines in your room.
- ☑ Find the free-form shape around the teddy bear.
- ☑ Find the curved line around the basketball.
- ☑ Find the square on the red box.
- ☑ The top of the can is an ellipse, not a circle or a straight line. An ellipse is a flattened circle with rounded ends. The curved line of an ellipse narrows at the ends. It does not have points.
- ☑ Find another ellipse in the photo. The width of an ellipse changes depending upon your view of it.

PRACTICE

Find an ellipse in your classroom. Practice drawing ellipses. Experiment with wide and narrow ellipses. Then, practice drawing objects with ellipses from different points of view.

More About...
Drawing People

People are made of free-form shapes. These shapes change depending upon what position a person is in.

More About...
Drawing People

LOOK

Look at the three people in the photograph. Notice the shape and size of the heads, necks, torsos, arms, legs, hands, and feet. These are free-form shapes.

✓ How are the walking person's arms and legs bending?

✓ Where does the sitting person's body bend?

✓ The standing person's feet are pointing toward you. These are like vertical ovals.

✓ How is the shape of the person's head that's sitting sideways different from the head of a person who is facing you? The person's head facing you is like an oval. The person's head facing sideways is a free-form.

✓ The back of the head is a large curve that goes in at the neck.

✓ The face has a nose, mouth, and chin that curve in and out.

✓ In this view, notice that the eye is almost a triangle with a curve at the front of the eyeball.

PRACTICE

Look at the people in your classroom. Can you find the same shapes and curves on their heads as you saw in the photograph? Practice drawing heads facing you. Practice drawing heads facing sideways.

More About...
Drawing Landscapes

When you look at a landscape, you can see that some things are in front of or behind other things.

More About...
Drawing Landscapes

LOOK

Look at the landscape with the horses.

- ☑ Look at the large horse in the **foreground,** the front of the picture. You cannot see part of the horse because the colt is in front of it, or **overlaps** it.
- ☑ Look at the horse in the **background,** the back of the picture.
- ☑ The area between the foreground and background is the **middle ground.** It is in the center of the paper. Find the horses in the middle ground. They look smaller than the horses in the foreground. They appear larger than the horse in the background.

The difference in the appearance of the horses' sizes gives the picture depth. The horse in the foreground is larger because it is closer. Things that are farther away appear smaller.

PRACTICE

Practice drawing foreground, middle ground, and background. Draw a large, tall object near the bottom of your paper. Next, draw a smaller object near the middle of your paper. Finally, draw an even smaller object near the top of your paper.

Practice overlapping. Draw a new, smaller object peeking out from behind each of the other objects. This creates even more depth.

Visual Index

Artist unknown
Egyptian Cat
950–300 B.C.
page 115

Artist unknown
Grain Tower
206 B.C.–A.D. 8
page 123

Artist unknown
Model of a House
A.D. 25-220
page 122

Artist unknown
*Shiva as Lord of
the Dance*
Twelfth century
page 178

Artist unknown
*Carved Lacquer
Circular Tray*
Twelfth century
page 174

Artist unknown
Jaguar
1440–1852
page 114

Shen Zhou
*Ode to Pomegranate
and Melon Vine*
1506–1509
page 37

**Peter Bruegel the
Elder**
Children's Games
1560
page 24

Visual Index

Artist unknown
Turtle Shell Mask
Eighteenth century
page 118

Itō Jakuchū
Fúkurojin, the God of Longevity and Wisdom
1790
page 171

Artist unknown
Tree–house Folly
1714
page 167

Artist unknown
Figure from House Post, Maori, New Zealand
Nineteenth century
page 166

Yosa Buson
Landscape with a Solitary Traveler
1780
page 97

Artist unknown
Yeihl Nax'in Raven Screen
1830
page 84

Jean-Honoré Fragonard
Rodomonte and Mandricardo State their Case before Agramante
1780s
page 21

Artist unknown
Church Quinua
Nineteenth century
page 110

Visual Index

Katsushika Hokusai
Boy with a Flute
1822–1849
page 36

George Catlin
Buffalo Bull's Back Fat, Head Chief, Blood Tribe
1832
page 46

Artist unknown
Face Mask
Nineteenth - twentieth centuries
page 119

Artist unknown
Ceremonial Shield
1852
page 88

Artist unknown
Canister
c. 1825
page 85

Henri-Julien-Félix Rousseau
Carnival Evening
1886
page 96

Katsushika Hokusai
Kajikaawa from *The Thirty-six Views of Fuji*
1828–1829
page 58

Henri de Toulouse-Lautrec
Le Jockey
1899
page 89

Visual Index

Artist unknown
Woodblock
Late 1800s
page 55

Henri Rousseau
Exotic Landscape
1910
page 157

Artist unknown
Osage Wedding Dress
Nineteenth century
page 152

Marc Chagall
Birthday
1915
page 66

Artist unknown
Osage Wedding Hat
Nineteenth century
page 153

M. C. Escher
Three Worlds
c. 1920
page 156

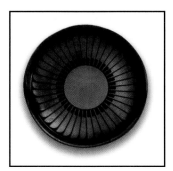

**Maria Martínez
and Popovi Da**
*Pottery Plate, Black
on Black Feather
Design*
c. 1910
page 175

Joseph Stella
*The White
Way I*
1920
page 16

Visual Index

Joaquin Torres-Garcia
New York City—Bird's-Eye View
c. 1920
page 140

Ralph Steiner
American Rural Baroque
1930
page 81

Simon Rodia
Watts Towers
1921–1959
page 126

Grant Wood
The Birthplace of Herbert Hoover
1931
page 136

Berthe Morisot
Woman at Her Toilette
1875
page 80

Diego M. Rivera
Detroit Industry, South Wall
1932–1933
page 144

Jacques Lipchitz
Reclining Figure with Guitar
1928
page 107

Diego M. Rivera
Detroit Industry, South Wall (detail)
1932–1933
page 145

Visual Index

Stuart Davis
Composition
1935
page 50

Henri Matisse
Les glaleuls. Study for Poesies de Stephane Mallarme
1931–1932
page 28

Emily Carr
Sky
1936
page 92

Joan Miró
Symbols and Love: Constellations of a Woman
1941
page 62

Antonio Ruíz
Bicycle Race, Texcoco
1938
page 137

Richard Pousette-Dart
Within the Room
1942
page 63

Stuart Davis
Report from Rockport
1940
page 77

Fred Kabotie
Hopi Tashaf Kachina Dance
1946
page 67

Visual Index

Henry Moore
Family Group
1948–1949
page 106

Audrey Flack
Self-Portrait
(*the Memory*)
1958
page 20

Enrique Grau
Niño con Paraguas
1964
page 93

Teodora Blanco
Woman
1965
page 111

Michael Naranjo
Eagle's Song
c. 1965
page 148

Visual Index

John Biggers
Shotgun, Third Ward #1
1966
page 47

Javacheff Christo and Jeanne-Claude
Running Fence
1972–1976
page 183

Minnie Evans
Design Made at Airlie Gardens
1967
page 51

Mark Uqayuittuq
Friendly Spirits
1972
page 29

Paul Goodnight
Endangered Species
c. 1970
page 25

Nancy Holt
Sun Tunnels
1973–1976
page 182

Visual Index

Benny Andrews
The Scholar
1974
page 32

Artist unknown
Hand-Stamped Cloth
1983
page 54

Allen Houser
Coming of Age
1977
page 59

Nancy Graves
Cantileve
1983
page 179

Jessica Hines
*Spirit of Place
Series #26*
c. 1980
page 170

**Claes Oldenburg
and Coosje van
Bruggen**
*Spoon Bridge and
Cherry*
1985
page 187

Visual Index

Carmen Lomas Garza
Cakewalk
1987
page 141

Jaune Quick-to-See Smith
Rainbow
1989
page 17

Brower Hatcher
Prophecy of the Ancients
1988
page 186

Benny Andrews
Patriots
1991
page 33

David Hockney
Large Interior Los Angeles
1988
page 76

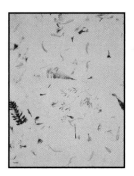

Jane Rhoades Hudak
Handmade Paper
1995
page 127

Glossary

additive sculpture
(ad´ i tiv skup´ chər), **noun**

A type of sculpture where something is added. The sculpture may be relief or freestanding.

alternating rhythm
(ôl´ tər nā ting   rith´ əm), **noun**

When the motif is changed in some way, a second motif is introduced, or the spaces between the motifs are changed.

analogous colors
(ə nal´ ə gəs kul´ ərz), **noun**

Colors that sit next to each other on the color wheel.

ant's view
(ants´ vū´), **noun**

Viewers feel they are looking up toward an object or figure.

assemblage
(ä säm bläzh´), **noun**

A technique in which an artist collects found materials and assembles them into a three-dimensional work of art.

asymmetry
(ā sim´i trē), **noun**

Another name for *informal balance.*

background
(bak´ ground´), **noun**

The part of the picture plane that seems to be farthest from the viewer.

bird's-eye view
(bûrdz´ ī   vū´), **noun**

Viewers feels they are looking down on a scene.

blind contour
(blīnd´   kon´ tür), **noun**

A type of drawing done by looking at the object being drawn and not at the paper.

close-up
(klōs´ up´), **noun**

Viewers feel they are right next to the object or are a part of the action in a picture.

color spectrum
(kul´ ər spek´ trəm), **noun**

The order of colors as they appear in natural light.

Glossary

color wheel
(kul´ ər hwēl´), **noun**

A circular chart organizing the colors of the spectrum.

complementary color scheme
(kom´ plə men tə rē kul´ ər skēm´), **noun**

A color scheme using one set of complementary colors.

complementary colors
(kom´ plə men tə rē kul´ ərz), **noun**

Colors that are opposite each other on the color wheel.

contour
(kon´ tŭr), **noun**

The edge or surface ridge of an object or figure.

contour drawing
(kon´ tŭr drô´ ing), **noun**

A drawing in which only contour lines are used.

contour lines
(kon´ tŭr līnz), **noun**

Lines that show the edges and surface ridges of an object.

contrast
(kon´ trast), **noun (verb)**

A difference between two things in an artwork.

curved
(kûrvd), **adj.**

Lines that bend and change direction slowly.

deckle
(dek´ əl), **noun**

A framed screen used for papermaking.

depth
(depth), **noun**

The appearance of distance on a flat surface.

diagonal
(dī ag´ ə nəl), **noun (adj.)**

A slanted line.

distortion
(di stôr´ shən), **noun**

When features of an object or person in a work of art are exaggerated and do not appear real.

dominant element
(dom´ ə nənt el´ ə mənt), **noun**

The element that is noticed first in a work of art.

emphasis
(em´ fə sis), **noun**

The principle of design that makes one part of the artwork stand out more than the other parts.

Glossary

environmental art
(en vī rən men´ təl ärt), **noun**

Art that is created to be part of a landscape.

faraway
(fär´ ə wā´), **adj.**

Viewers feel they are standing far away from the scene.

flowing rhythm
(flō´ ing rith´ əm), **noun**

Repeating curved lines or shapes.

foreground
(fôr´ ground´), **noun**

The part of the picture plane that appears closest to the viewer.

form
(fôrm), **noun**

A three-dimensional figure.

formal balance
(fôr´ məl bal´ əns), **noun**

A way of organizing parts of a design so that similar elements are placed on opposite sides of a central line.

found materials
(found´ mə tîr´ ē əlz), **noun**

Items found in your home, school, or outdoor environment that can be used to create a work of art.

free-form shape
(frē´ fôrm´ shāp´), **noun**

An irregular and uneven shape; any shape that is not geometric.

freestanding assemblage
(frē´ stan´ ding ä säm bläzh´), **noun**

A type of assemblage that has space all around it. Freestanding assemblage is meant to be viewed from all sides.

freestanding sculpture
(frē´ stan´ ding skulp´ chər), **noun**

A type of sculpture that is surrounded by space on all sides.

frozen motion
(frō´ zən mō´ shən), **noun**

When one action is "frozen" in time.

functional form
(fungk´ shə nəl fôrm´), **noun**

An object created by an artist for use in daily life.

geometric shape
(jē´ ə met´ rik shāp), **noun**

A figure that has precise measurements and can be described in mathematical terms.

gesture
(jes´ chər), **noun**

An expressive movement.

Glossary

gesture lines
(jes´ chər līnz), **noun**

Lines quickly drawn to capture the movement of a person, animal, or object in a painting or drawing.

gesture sketch
(jes´ chər skech), **noun**

A quick sketch to capture movement or action of a person, animal, or object.

harmony
(här mə nē), **noun**

The principle of design that creates unity by stressing similarities of separate but related parts.

horizontal
(hôr´ ə zon´ təl), **adj.**

A line that moves from side to side.

hue
(hū), **noun**

Another name for *color.*

implied line
(im plīd´ līn´), **noun**

A series of points that are connected by the viewer's eyes.

informal balance
(in fôr´məl bal´ əns), **noun**

A way of organizing parts of a design so that objects have equal visual weight.

intensity
(in ten´ si tē), **noun**

The brightness or dullness of a color.

intermediate color
(in´ tər mē´ dē it kul´ ər), **noun**

One of six colors that are made when a primary color is mixed with a secondary color.

invented texture
(in ven´ təd teks´ chər), **noun**

Visual texture of repeating lines and shapes in a two-dimensional pattern.

line
(līn), **noun**

A mark drawn by a tool such as a pencil, pen, or paintbrush as it moves across a surface.

line variation
(līn´ vâr´ ē ā´ shən), **noun**

Changes in the look of a line.

matte
(mat), **adj.**

Texture that reflects a soft and dull light.

middle ground
(mid´ əl ground´), **noun**

The area in a picture between the foreground and background.

minimal detail
(min´ ə məl di tāl´), **noun**

Very little detail in a drawing.

Glossary

monochromatic
(mon´ ə krō mat´ ik), **adj.**

Having one color.

monochromatic color scheme
(mon´ ə krō mat´ ik kul´ ər skēm´), **noun**

One color plus all the tints and shades of that color.

motif
(mō tēf´), **noun**

Something visual that is repeated in rhythm.

movement
(müv´ mənt), **noun**

Constant motion.

mural
(myür´ əl), **noun**

A large work of art painted onto a wall.

negative space
(neg´ ə tiv spās´), **noun**

The area around, under, above, inside, and between objects.

neutral color scheme
(nü trəl kul´ ər skēm), **noun**

A color scheme using black, white, and a variety of grays.

neutral colors
(nü trəl kul´ ərz), **noun**

Black, white, and gray.

nonobjective painting
(non´ əb jek´ tiv pān´ ting), **noun**

A painting with no recognizable subject matter.

observation brush drawing
(ob´ zər vā´ shən brush´ drô´ ing), **noun**

The first sketch done with brush and watercolors.

observation drawing
(ob´ zər vā´ shən drô´ ing), **noun**

A drawing made while looking at a person or object.

overlap
(ō´ vər lap´), **verb (noun)**

When one object covers part of a second object, the first seems to be closer to the viewer.

perception
(pər sep´ shən), **noun**

The way you look or think about what you see.

perspective
(pər spek´ tiv), **noun**

The technique used to create the feeling of depth on a flat surface.

perspective techniques
(pər spek´ tiv tek nēks´), **noun**

Techniques used by artists to create the feeling of depth on a flat surface.

Glossary

picture plane
(pik´ chər plān´), **noun**

The surface of a drawing or painting.

point of view
(point´ əv vū´), **noun**

The angle from which the viewer sees an object.

position
(pə zish´ ən), **noun (verb)**

The placement of elements in a work of art.

positive space
(poz´ i tiv spās´), **noun**

The figure, shape, or object.

primary color
(prī´ mer ē kul´ ər), **noun**

A basic color that cannot be mixed with other colors to make it. Red, yellow, and blue are primary colors.

progressive motion
(prə gres´ iv mō shən), **noun**

When a scene or motif changes a little each time it is repeated.

proportion
(prə pôr´ shən), **noun**

Relation of one object to another in size and placement so that objects in a work of art appear real.

radial balance
(rā dē əl bal´ əns), **noun**

When the elements in a design come out from one central point.

radiate
(rā dē āt´), **verb**

To come out from a central point.

random rhythm
(ran´ dəm ri<u>th</u>´ əm), **noun**

Motifs that appear in no apparent order and have irregular spaces in between.

regular rhythm
(reg´ yə lər ri<u>th</u>´ əm), **noun**

Identical motifs with equal amounts of space between them.

relief assemblage
(ri lēf´ ä säm bläzh´), **noun**

A type of assemblage where objects stick out from one side only.

relief sculpture
(ri lēf´ skulp´ chər), **noun**

A type of sculpture where objects stick out from a flat surface.

repeated lines
(ri pēt´ əd līnz´), **noun**

Lines used to give the feeling of movement or motion.

repeated shapes
(ri pēt´ əd shāps´), **noun**

Shapes that are repeated to give the feeling of motion.

Glossary

rhythm
(ri<u>th</u>ʹ əm), **noun**

The repetition of lines, shapes, or colors to create a feeling of movement.

rough
(ruf), **adj.**

Texture that reflects light unevenly.

sculpture
(skulpʹ chər), **noun**

A type of three-dimensional art.

secondary color
(sekʹ ən derʹ ē kulʹ ər), **noun**

Two primary colors mixed together. Orange, green, and violet are secondary colors.

shade
(shād), **noun**

Any dark value of a color.

shape
(shāp), **noun**

A flat, two-dimensional figure. Shapes can be measured only by height and width.

shiny
(shīʹ nē), **adj.**

Texture that reflects a bright light.

silhouette
(silʹ ü etʹ), **noun**

The shape of a shadow.

simplicity
(sim plisʹ i tē), **noun**

Limiting the number of elements in an artwork.

simulated texture
(simʹ ū lāʹ təd teksʹ chər), **noun**

A kind of visual texture that imitates real texture by using a two-dimensional pattern to create the illusion of a three-dimensional surface.

smooth
(smü<u>th</u>), **adj.**

Texture that reflects light evenly.

spectral color scheme
(spekʹ trəl kulʹ ər skēmʹ), **noun**

A color scheme using all the colors of the spectrum.

still life
(stilʹ līfʹ), **noun**

A picture of things that do not move.

subtractive sculpture
(səb trakʹ tiv skulpʹ chər), **noun**

A type of sculpture made from carving a form. The original material is taken away, or subtracted.

Glossary

symmetry

(sim´ i trē), **noun**

A type of formal balance in which two halves of an object or composition are mirror images of each other.

tactile texture

(tak´ təl teks´ chər), **noun**

The element of art that refers to how things actually feel.

three-dimensional

(thrē´ di men´ shə nəl), **adj. (noun)**

Something that can be measured by height, width, and depth.

tint

(tint), **noun**

Any light value of a color.

two-dimensional

(tü´ di men´ shə nəl), **adj. (noun)**

Something that can be measured only by height and width.

two-dimensional shape

(tü´ di men´ shə nəl shāp´), **noun**

A flat figure that can be measured only by length and width.

unity

(ū´ ni tē), **noun**

The feeling of oneness or wholeness in a work of art.

value

(val´ ū), **noun**

The lightness or darkness of a color.

variety

(və rī´ ə tē), **noun**

Differences and contrasts in a work of art.

vertical

(vûr´ tə kəl), **adj.**

A line that moves up and down.

visual movement

(vizh´ ü əl müv´ mənt), **noun**

The rhythm of repeated lines, shapes, and colors to create a sense of movement.

visual rhythm

(vizh´ ü əl ri<u>th</u>´ əm), **noun**

Rhythm in art you see, created by the repetition of lines, shapes, and colors.

visual texture

(vizh´ ü əl teks´ chər), **noun**

Texture you can see with your eyes.

visual weight

(vizh´ ü əl wāt´), **noun**

The weight of elements in a work of art seen, not measured.

zigzag

(zig´ zag´), **adj.**

Diagonal lines that connect and change direction sharply.

Index

Index

Index

Index

Index